EXPLORERS

EXPLORERS

Journeys to the Ends of the Earth

JON BALCHIN

ARCTURUS

This edition published in 2014 by Arcturus Publishing Limited
26/27 Bickels Yard, 151–153 Bermondsey Street,
London SE1 3HA

Copyright © 2005 Arcturus Publishing Limited
Originally published as 'To the Ends of the Earth'

AD003886EN

Printed in the UK

Contents

CONTENTS

Chapter 1

BEYOND THE PILLARS OF HERCULES:

The Discovery of Europe

Europe is the forgotten continent of exploration. In the rush to recall the myriad glorious expeditions that departed her shores in order to unveil the world, history often neglects the earlier exploration of Europe itself.

Long before the lands that are now the modern day states of Europe were 'discovered' there were, of course, native populations to be found there. And the Americas, Africa, Asia and Australia were also populated before they were unveiled by explorers. When we say that these and the other continents that are encompassed in this book have been 'discovered', then, we mean that they have been 'brought' to the attention of the wider world. Consequently, the individuals who have achieved this feat, often through great personal hardship, are celebrated as 'explorers' and 'discoverers'.

Many of the world's great explorers came from Europe. Yet before moving on to reveal the rest of the world, adventurers from this region first had their own continent to uncover. Why journey to Asia when the Adriatic was still to be conquered? How could the North Pole be contemplated when the North of France remained out of reach? Hundreds of years before Christ, European discoverers were attempting to answer these questions so that their descendants could grab the globe two millennia later, unhindered by such trivial considerations.

Colaeus of Samos *Seventh century BC*

One of the earliest of these discoverers was Colaeus of Samos, explorer of the Atlantic Ocean. At the time of his great, if largely accidental, voyage of around 630 BC, 'known' Europe was dominated by two civilisations, the Greeks and the Phoenicians. Both had settlements that hugged the beaches of the Mediterranean, so it is from this sea that the history of the exploration of Europe begins.

The Phoenicians came originally from present day Lebanon, but for several centuries from around 1,000 BC onwards they opened up colonies along the African and European coastlines of the Mediterranean, until their principal focus was to the west. The Greeks by contrast dominated the east side of the sea, down as far as Egypt and up into the Black Sea. Both races were great traders as well as navigators, so both were protective of their areas of influence as much for commercial as for political reasons.

Colaeus's achievement of being the first Greek to view the Atlantic is all the more impressive, then, because he had to pass through the Phoenician sphere of influence on the way. He had not necessarily intended it that way. Sailing from the Greek territory of Samos, he had merely been trying to reach Egypt on what was probably a trading mission. A tremendous storm, though, blew him not just a few miles off course but right across the western Mediterranean. Possibly managing to stop briefly somewhere off the coast of Libya, Colaeus remained powerless to prevent his ship from being blown all the way to the 'Pillars of Hercules'. Today, the small passage where the Mediterranean meets the Atlantic is called the 'Strait of Gibraltar' but then, as far as the Greeks were concerned, it represented the edge of the known world.

Having gone so far off course, Colaeus, sharing the curiosity of all great explorers, could not resist pushing through the Pillars into the vast Atlantic beyond. Breaking through this barrier would have been as much a psychological as a physical achievement for the Greeks, who feared the immense unfamiliar waters, waves and perhaps sea monsters that lay on the other side.

Having sailed the Strait, Colaeus explored the southwestern coastline of modern Spain. He stopped at Gades (present day Cádiz) and traded with the people of a territory then known as Tartessus. This population had overland trading contacts with Europeans from further north, which allowed them to control the flow of metals, such as tin, that could be sourced there.

Himilco *c.fifth century BC*

Not to be outdone by the Greeks, the Phoenicians had established a fine reputation for themselves as explorers, traders and colonisers. One of their more significant settlements was Carthage, or Carthago, in what is now Tunis, where they could access gold from across Africa. In time, after the fall of their 'home' territories in the eastern Mediterranean to the Assyrians, Carthage would become an increasingly important colony for the Phoenicians. Indeed, the 'Carthaginians' began identifying themselves as a people and a civilisation in their own right, looking to dominate the western Mediterranean and to explore beyond. Enter Himilco, a Carthaginian sent out with orders 'to explore the outer coasts of Europe'.

The motivation for Himilco's historic voyage was almost certainly commerce. Once beyond the Phoenician settlement of Gades (Cádiz) in southwest Spain, he was ordered to travel north to territories which had never been visited by the Carthaginians but were known to exist because the Spanish civilisation of Tartessus indirectly obtained tin from there. As aggressive traders, the Carthaginians would almost certainly have preferred to control this metal supply themselves. What better way to achieve such an end than to bypass the middleman altogether and discover the source of the tin directly? Such was Himilco's task.

It took Himilco almost four months to journey to the 'Oestrumnides', sailing with perhaps as many as sixty ships in his fleet. He probably made many stops in uncharted territory along the way, thereby explaining the reasonably lengthy amount of time it took him to make the journey to the 'Tin Islands'. It is not entirely clear where the Oestrumnides were: they could possibly have been situated as far north as Cornwall in England, but it is more likely that they were either the Isles of Scilly, just off the British coast, or were in Brittany, France.

Whatever the actual location, Himilco returned to tell the tale: he was the first Carthaginian to reach northwestern Europe, and one of the first people in history to record details of these lands. Indeed, in spite of the Carthaginians' secretive nature, Himilco wrote a thorough account of his voyage which has subsequently been lost to history. Because of this, modern knowledge of his feats has been passed on through secondary authors, such as the first century Roman writer Pliny the Elder and the fourth century scribe Rufus Festus

Avienus. The stories of Colaeus and others were later relayed through another particularly significant author, Herodotus, the fifth century BC Greek historian.

Pytheas *Fifth century BC*

Similarly, the accounts of another great early European explorer, Pytheas, have also only been passed on through secondary sources. As the first known explorer of certain areas of northwestern Europe he recorded his feats in a text called *On The Ocean*, but over time it too was lost. Consequently, some of the details of his extraordinary journey, as relayed by others, are unclear. What is known is that he almost certainly went further north than any other Mediterranean-based explorer had been before.

Pytheas's voyage began from the French port of Marseilles, then called Massilia, in c.325 BC. His aim was to head west and then north, probably under the patronage of a rich merchant in search of amber or tin. Even the details of this early part of his journey, though, are unclear. In order to protect their trade interests against foreigners, the Carthaginians had imposed a blockade on the Pillars of Hercules, which meant that it would have been extremely difficult for Pytheas, as a Greek, to exit the western Mediterranean. It is possible that he travelled under cover of darkness and, with great care, managed to avoid detection via this route. Others have speculated, however, that he journeyed overland through what is now France, avoiding the Strait of Gibraltar altogether by entering the sea to the west of that country.

Through one of these methods, Pytheas eventually arrived in what is now Cornwall in present-day Britain, a place rich in the tin he was almost certainly seeking. Far from simply returning with the spoils of his mission, though, Pytheas had only just begun his journey. The explorer's next step was to circumnavigate the British Isles. It is likely that Pytheas also investigated much of the country by land and river, thereby becoming one of the first outsiders to observe the customs and lifestyles of its native inhabitants.

During this period, Pytheas heard of a land called Thule that was six days journey to the north of Britain. He set off to find it and later describes his arrival on the fabled 'island'. Even today we are uncertain as to exactly where he landed. Common opinion has it that Pytheas probably ended up in Norway, although competing theories suggest that the Faroe Islands, the Shetlands,

Iceland or even Greenland could have been his destination.

Still, Pytheas had not satisfied his craving for discovery. He proceeded 'Ultima Thule', or to the far north, which was at least another day's sailing from the 'island'. Extracts from his writings that have been passed on by other authors vividly describe the increasing difficulty of his journey: encountering ice and thick fog, he pushed forward the bounds of exploration. Eventually, he was forced by the hostile conditions to turn south and sail for home. On the way it is possible that he explored other areas of the North Sea, perhaps even heading into the Baltic Sea.

The end of Pytheas's journey is as much a mystery as the beginning. Again, it is unclear as to whether he made it back to Marseilles through mainland France or via the sea route. When he did return, though, he was mocked for the account he offered of his fantastic voyage. Instead, it would require the passage of time and the efforts of later Greek writers to cement his place in the history of European exploration.

Gardar Svavarsson and Naddod *Ninth century*

More than a thousand years later, another wave of great adventurers, the Vikings, emerged to push the edges of European exploration to its extremes. The Scandinavians had already conquered many previously settled countries on the continent in the latter centuries of the first millennium, but now they began finding new territory too. It was not always intentional, though, as was the case when they discovered Europe's westernmost land, Iceland.

Alternative accounts credit two different Vikings with reaching Iceland first. Some record Gardar Svavarsson, a Swede who later settled in Norway, as the first Viking to arrive. Others claim the finding for Naddod, a Norwegian chief and traveller. In truth, the first people to reach Iceland were quite possibly some Irish monks, a century or so before the Vikings, who probably went there to seek peaceful sanctuary. If they were still around when the Scandinavians arrived (that is, if they were ever there at all), then they did not remain for too much longer.

So it is the Vikings who are recorded as the discoverers of Iceland; certainly, they were the first to bring it into popular Western consciousness. Most conventional accounts suggest that Naddod arrived first, probably in around 861. He had been attempting to reach the Faroe Islands from Norway but was blown off course during a storm. Consequently he drifted to the east coast of Iceland. He probably stayed there for a few months before returning to the Faroes. Noting the fact that the peaks of many of the mountains retained their white covering throughout the year, he initially gave this new country the name of 'Snowland'.

It is believed by some that Naddod's positive account of his discovery acted as an inspiration for Gardar Svavarsson to also seek out the same territory in around 864. Others, however, record Svavarsson as having had an experience that was as serendipitous as Naddod's, by being blown off course there while trying to reach the Hebrides at around the time of, or perhaps even before, Naddod's discovery. While this is not clear, Svavarsson almost certainly took his exploration further by circumnavigating the island and then spending the winter there. In order to survive the harsh environment, Svavarsson and his men built huts in the north of the island and named the settlement 'Husavik' (Bay of Houses). He also named Iceland after himself, calling it 'Gardarsholmur' (Gardar's Island). Inadvertently, Svavarsson's expedition also left behind the first settlers on the island, although how long they survived is unknown. Whereas Gardar's party returned after a year or so to Norway, his slave Nattfari and one or two others were left behind, either because they escaped or by accident.

Others soon came in an attempt to make a more permanent settlement on the island, however, beginning with Floki Vilgerdarson, another Norwegian explorer. It was through him that the country was given the name that it retains to this day. Vilgerdarson observed that ice remained in the country's fjords for much of the year and decided that Iceland was, therefore, a more appropriate name than Naddod's Snowland or Svavarsson's Gardarsholmur.

It stuck. Sadly for Floki, his settlement at Vatnsfjord Bay did not. Although he imported livestock and fellow travellers in a bid to make his stay a permanent one, he was apparently so engaged in Iceland's abundant fishing during the summer that he forgot to prepare hay for the winter. Consequently, all of his cattle perished during the coldest, most barren months and Vilgerdarson himself barely survived. He was so put off by the harshness of the environment and his sour experiences that he soon left, never to return.

The first successful settlement in Iceland did not take place until around 874. Ingolfur Arnarson arrived there with his family and some others, following a dispute with local chiefs back in his native Norway. He ended up residing on the southeastern side of the island, in a place he named Reykjavik, meaning Smoky Bay. Reykjavik remains the capital city of Iceland to this day.

Ottar *Ninth century*

So the Vikings had reached Europe's westernmost territory, but one question that continued to remain unanswered was just how far north did mainland Europe stretch? Another Scandinavian, by the name of Ottar, soon became the first known explorer to solve this conundrum in around 890. Part of Ottar's advantage lay in the fact that he began his famous journey from an extremely northerly position in the first place. Indeed, in the account he dictated, he claimed to have departed from a settlement which already lay 'north of all the Northmen'. This was in an area known as Halgoland, which lies in Troms county on the northwest coast of modern day Norway.

Ottar was curious to know just how far to the north

the land stretched, as well as wanting to investigate the hunting possibilities in the territory, perhaps for walruses. Indeed, his vast wealth, by Viking standards, depended very much on hunting and animals, because he owned over 600 reindeer, as well as cattle, sheep and pigs. In addition, Ottar, or Ohthere as he is also sometimes called, was a great trader, which boosted his riches and fame still further.

It was this celebrity that ultimately resulted in the recording of his northward exploits. Ottar was so well known that King Alfred of Wessex in England asked for an audience with him during a trade visit to the Isles. At the time, Alfred was updating an old Roman history of the known world from AD 400, with details of additional discoveries and advances over the ensuing 500 years. The King was so impressed by the details of Ottar's adventure that he recorded them in *The Old English Orosius*, the account through which we know of the Viking's achievement today.

Having resolved to answer the northerly question, Ottar left his home by boat. He sailed six days to the north, including three days beyond waters that had already been charted by whale hunters. Observing only wasteland as he travelled, Ottar eventually arrived at what is now known as the North Cape, Europe's northernmost point. His journey did not stop there, however, because he picked up a wind that carried him four days to the east. Finally, he followed the land south into the White Sea for a further five days until he arrived at the mouth of the River Dvina. Ottar had rounded the top of Norway and Finland and sailed to where the port of Archangel now lies in present-day Russia.

Ottar turned back at this point, for he encountered the permanent settlements of the Biarmians on the left-hand side of the river, whom he feared might attack him. This was the first community he had encountered on his journey, thereby confirming his assumption that he did indeed live 'north of all the Northmen'. The only other people he had seen amongst the wastelands of the far north were occasional hunters, bird catchers and fishermen. He later claimed that the Biarmians told him stories of unknown lands, but he would not pass these details on to Alfred because Ottar had not been there himself and could not, therefore, verify their accuracy. Similarly, Ottar did not have the opportunity to push on further south into the White Sea in order to explore his incorrect belief that Scandinavia was an island.

Instead, he triumphantly returned from his conquest of the north as a Nordic legend. One of the last of Europe's secrets had been unveiled. Future explorers from the continent could now concentrate their efforts on 'revealing' the rest of the world.

Chapter 2

IN ALEXANDER'S FOOTSTEPS:
Opening up Asia

A popular notion of the history of Asian
exploration begins with Marco Polo peeping
through the continent's keyhole, and then little
else of significance occurring until Vasco da Gama
firmly wedged open the door a couple of centuries
later. At best, though, this is a simplified view of
actual events; at worst it borders on untruthfulness.

For more than a thousand years before Polo, Asia was already being actively explored, conquered and opened up for trade from all sides. Alexander the Great came from the west and the Chinese came from the east. Egypt sent her pioneers from the south and, in the meantime, vast empires such as that of Persia had been flourishing. In addition, countless nameless merchants from Central Asia and the Middle East had been the established lynchpin in East–West trade for centuries before the European colonisers came along.

Ibn Battuta *(1304–1369)*

Yet even conceding that Polo was among the first people to give a new, 'refreshed' glimpse of Asia to the wider world, at least two less famous explorers followed the Venetian before da Gama came along. Their feats deserve to be just as celebrated. The first of these was Ibn Battuta in the fourteenth century. A Moroccan from Tangiers, his achievements are remarkable for many reasons but above all, perhaps, for the sheer distance that he covered at a time when the available methods of transport were very primitive. Even today, few could ever cover the 75,000 miles of territory that he traversed, much of which remained cut off to Europeans for many more centuries.

Battuta was fortunate in that his affluent family background and subsequent education in law gave him the financial opportunity to travel. Once he had seized his chance, though, he took the concept of exploration to a level that had been rarely, if ever, seen. In simple distance terms, the Muslim Battuta completely surpassed his European predecessor, Polo.

Indeed, it was Battuta's faith that was very much at the heart of his urge to travel. Once he had returned to Morocco after three decades on the road, Battuta dictated the details of his journey to an author named Ibn Juzay al-Kalbi. As much as it was a travelogue in its own right, the resultant book, *Rihla*, was also a tribute to the size and influence of the Muslim world at that time, for Battuta had visited every one of the states within it at some point. The Islamic lands stretched through Africa, the Middle East, Southern Europe and, of course, Asia, and its trading and maritime influence extended even further. Battuta took the opportunity his journeys provided him to witness it all at first hand.

He began, appropriately, with a pilgrimage through

northern Africa to Mecca in 1325. Battuta would return there many times during his travels. Indeed, after an excursion from Mecca into Iraq and Persia, he spent another three years in the Holy City before moving on. When he finally left, he journeyed by water along the coast of East Africa, travelling as far as Tanzania, at a time when Africa was also very much an unknown quantity to European explorers. Eventually turning northwards again, Battuta circled the Arabian Peninsula by sea before landing somewhere along the Persian Gulf coast, from where he again made his way to Mecca. It was at this point that Battuta's Asian adventures began in earnest, when he chose to head northwards first before turning east. In the process he crossed the Black Sea and reached as far as what is now present-day Istanbul. He then travelled through the states bordering the north side of the Black and Caspian Seas and worked his way through Central Asia into India.

The Indian subcontinent would become another favoured destination of Battuta's, where he found employment as a judge in the service of the Muslim Sultan Mohammad Tughlaq of Delhi. After working for him for the best part of a decade, Battuta was sent on an official mission to China. Opting to take the sea route, Battuta passed through the Maldives, Ceylon, Eastern India, Sumatra and Malaya on the way to Canton. On reaching China, he possibly travelled as far north as what is now Beijing. Eventually, Battuta would begin his homeward journey, again by sea, through southern Asia, India and back into the Middle East. He returned to Mecca once more before heading home to Morocco, where he arrived in 1349, some quarter of a century after he had left. Even now, though, the Moroccan had not lost his travel itch. He would also visit southern Spain and, remarkably, cross the Sahara Desert to Timbuktu before ending his trekking days.

Cheng Ho *(1371–1435)*

The other pre-da Gama notable was the fifteenth century Chinese adventurer, Cheng Ho, also known as San Bao. Nearly a hundred years before European ships arrived in numbers in Asia, China was undertaking similarly enormous fleet voyages off the Asian and East African coastlines. It was an enterprise that soon made China the dominant power across the whole region and Cheng Ho was at the heart of it.

Cheng Ho undertook at least seven major expeditions, and possibly more, on the orders of the Ming dynasty Emperor Ch'eng Tsu. The Emperor was keen to establish diplomatic relations with as many foreign countries as possible. This would not only extend the reach and influence of Chinese authority but also increase the possibility of enjoying trade, wealth and imported luxury items.

So it was that Cheng Ho began his first expedition in 1405, with some 300 ships and nearly 28,000 men under his command. The sixty or so flagships in the fleet were enormous, each being some 400 feet long and dwarfing the ships of most of the European entourages that came a century later. The vessels were laden with gifts for foreign rulers and items to trade with a view to helping Cheng Ho's mission prosper. Consequently, the Chinese Admiral's two-year voyage around the South China Sea, into Java, Ceylon and India was a complete success, resulting in new imports and new international friends.

Encouraged by this, the Emperor would keep Cheng Ho busy on the seas for the next two decades. As well as making trips to previously visited countries and journeying to many new destinations in Southeast Asia such as Siam, Malaysia and the Philippines, Cheng Ho's reach also extended far to the west. His missions extended to the Persian Gulf and Arabia, including a pilgrimage to Mecca which, as a Muslim, Cheng Ho was keen to undertake. Furthermore, the expeditions stretched on to Egypt and the coastline of East Africa where many important relations were established. Indeed, ambassadors from up to thirty countries returned to China with Cheng Ho, thereby cementing political relations.

Some commentators believe that one of Cheng Ho's expeditions made it around the Cape of Good Hope, Africa's southern tip, in around 1420, more than half a century before the Portuguese managed the same feat from Europe. Maps showing some of the west coast of Africa, possibly from this period, back up this claim. There are other reports of Cheng Ho describing French, Portuguese and Dutch people, so there is a remote possibility, therefore, that he might even have reached the shores of Europe. There is even some small evidence that Cheng Ho's fleets discovered America, decades before Columbus. Again, advocates point to possible maps from the period which mark out the continent. More likely is the probability that one of his fleets reached the northern Australian coastline, centuries before other more famous explorers.

The Emperor Ch'eng Tsu died towards the end of Cheng Ho's expeditionary period and with his death went much of China's interest in the internationalism he had practised. China became increasingly isolationist to the point where, only a few years after Cheng Ho's own death, it turned its back on the outside world completely. China abandoned the cultural, technological and economic dominance it had established across Asia, the Middle East and East Africa, leaving the door open for European colonists a few decades later.

In spite of this, and the fact that many of his records were subsequently destroyed, Cheng Ho's achievements paved the way for others. In particular, much of the ancient 'Silk Road' traffic had moved to and remained on the 'Sea Silk Road', as countries in the region took advantage of the new opportunities to trade. So when da Gama sailed into Asia for the first time he was, in fact, already gliding into nearly a century of established commercial routes. And this, of course, was in addition to some two thousand years of wider knowledge of the

Asian domain that had been established by even earlier Asian explorers.

Alexander the Great *(356–323 BC)* and the early Asian explorers

Alexander the Great was by no means a conventional explorer. But then neither was he a conventional man. In many respects his inclusion in this book under the title 'explorer' is something of an indulgence, but such were the distances he covered and amount of countries he reached so early in history and in such a short space of time, that it is impossible to ignore his single-minded feats.

A Macedonian, Alexander became king of his home country at the age of twenty. By thirty-three, he was dead. In the intervening thirteen years he had created the largest empire in history and personally visited most of the territory within it. Indeed, he had personally led the conquest of much of it.

Yet while Alexander was undeniably a ruthless leader, his explorations and conquests were, in many respects, driven by a much softer, loftier ideal. Educated by Aristotle and accustomed to meeting foreigners at the court of his father and predecessor, King Philip II of Macedonia, Alexander had a broad view of the world from an early age. Rather than stamp out the diversity of the world, he was keen to embrace it. Consequently, his desire was to unify the whole of the known world into a single country that combined the best elements of East and West in its governance and culture. He very nearly achieved it.

After ascending to the Macedonian throne, the first act of the young king was to unite Greece behind him, putting down a number of uprisings in the process. An early example of his ruthless streak was when he ransacked the city of Thebes after a revolt. In the process his army destroyed every building in the city except for its temples and the homes of a famous poet called Pindar. Many were killed in the process and the thousands of surviving inhabitants were sold into slavery by the king. It was an example which ensured that the other towns of Greece soon fell into line behind him.

By this stage, Alexander had already engaged in a brief foray against the Persian army but his ultimate aim was to implement what had initially been his father's plan and obliterate it. To do this, Alexander embarked on a remarkable decade-long journey which would take him across Asia. He began by working his way through Asia Minor, continually overcoming the resistance put up by the armies of the Persian King Darius III. He proceeded through Syria before entering Egypt, where he was welcomed as a liberator from Persian rule. One of his most enduring legacies there was to found and name the city of Alexandria in 331 BC. He journeyed as far west as Libya before turning his attentions back to Persia once more.

Again he defeated Darius, this time in Mesopotamia at the Battle of Gaugamela, before marching on to Babylon. Over the next years he proceeded through the rest of Persia, during which time Darius was murdered for his crown by his own cousin Bessus. He did not keep it for long, for Alexander soon caught and executed him, securing his own claim as King of Persia.

Still, Alexander's thirst for new territory was not quenched. He proceeded on through what is now Afghanistan, then extended his dominance into northern India. He then had a fleet of ships built and sailed down the River Indus to its mouth. With his men weary of further expansion and the threat of mutiny in the air,

Alexander opted to consolidate his empire by sending his fleet along a little-explored sea route to the Persian Gulf. He marched the rest of his army through desert terrain in what is now Pakistan and Iran and met his fleet again at Susa.

The next year, Alexander headed back up to Babylon, which he had selected to be the new capital of his enormous empire. There he planned governmental and administrative reforms, as well as a sea expedition around the Arabian peninsula. Sadly for Alexander, this would be one journey that was just too far out of reach. A few weeks later, at the height of his power and empire, Alexander caught what was probably malaria and died shortly afterwards.

Alexander's enormous empire crumbled rapidly into disarray after his untimely death. It had been so quick in the making and his death so sudden, that there had been no time to groom a successor or bed in the administrative institutions which were required to manage such a vast territory. Yet while the governmental pillars of the empire disintegrated, much of the social and ritual fabric remained, most noticeably in the lasting permeation of Hellenic cultural influences across the region.

Chang Ch'ien *(c.160–c.107 BC)*

The spirit of exploration had soon spread across the whole of Asia. Within a couple of centuries, the Chinese were knocking on the door of the eastern end of Alexander's former empire with their own investigations. One of her citizens, Chang Ch'ien (or Zhang Qian as he is sometimes called) is credited with being the founder of the 'Silk Road', a great trading route that linked China to Central Asia and the West.

Chang Ch'ien's explorations were initially motivated by military concerns, initially without much success. The Emperor of China at that time, Wu Ti (who ruled from 140–87 BC), was keen to make alliances with those who shared his common enemy, 'the Huns' (known then as the Hsiung-nu or Xiongnu). The Huns, a nomadic people, regularly made raids on China from the northwest. A tribe called the Yueh-chih had also suffered at the hands of the Huns. Living on the opposite edge of Hun territory from the Chinese, they had been forcibly pushed even further west by the invasions of their shared enemy.

Consequently, Wu Ti decided that it would be a sound strategy to attempt to befriend the Yüeh-chih and so he decided to send an envoy into those largely unexplored and dangerous lands in an attempt to establish diplomatic relations. Chang Ch'ien, who worked for the Emperor as a commander at the Imperial Palace in the then capital, Chang'an (or Xian), volunteered for the mission. Wu Ti gave him a hundred men to take with him and in 138 BC they began their mission. It would be another thirteen years before Chang Ch'ien returned.

The main reason for the long duration of the voyage was that the great Chinese explorer spent up to eleven of those years in captivity. He had taken a northern passage through Hun territory en route to the Yüeh-chih in the hope of avoiding capture. Unfortunately, he was not only caught but he also spent the next decade as a Hun prisoner. During this time, however, he married a local woman and had a son with her before finally escaping and continuing his journey westwards.

Eventually, he made it to the capital of the Yüeh-chih people in what is now Afghanistan. By this time, however, the tribe had abandoned their previously nomadic ways, along with their desire to return to the lands from which the Huns had driven them, and were settled in their new territory. Consequently, there was no desire for a military alliance which would potentially bring them into a conflict in which they were no longer interested.

After taking eleven years to get there, Chang Ch'ien had failed in his diplomatic mission. Now he had to return home to break the news to Wu Ti. This time he took a southern passage near Tibet in an attempt to avoid recapture by the Huns. Again, Chang Ch'ien failed. He spent another year in captivity with his wife and son before escaping with them for a second time.

Eventually, thirteen years after he had begun, Chang Ch'ien arrived back at Chang'an, accompanied by only one of his original one hundred men. Far more important than the news of the failed alliance, however, were the fascinating stories of the lands, cultures and routes he had explored on his way to and from the Yüeh-chih. Even more excitingly, he had heard stories of great civilisations even further to the west, the Persians, Mesopotamians and Romans, with whom possible new trading partnerships could be formed through the routes he had uncovered.

Chang Ch'ien was later sent on a second expedition in around 115 BC, with a similar goal of making a military alliance against the Huns with another western tribe, the Wu-sun. This in turn inspired Chang Ch'ien himself to send out envoys to places such as India, to investigate the possible establishment of other commercial and military partnerships.

Shortly after his return from his second expedition, Chang Ch'ien became ill and died. His actions and bravery had, however, already established a legacy that would help China trade profitably with other Asian countries for the next thousand years: the routes into Central Asia that Chang Ch'ien had discovered became part of the famous Silk Road trading route. From around 105 BC, and for centuries afterwards, major commercial cargoes containing, amongst other goods, spices and the much prized silk, began to be sent out along this land route from China into Central Asia and the Middle East. In turn these goods would often find their way into Europe and the Roman Empire, setting up the first East–West commercial dependencies. Soon goods and animals also began flowing in the opposite direction including horses, leather and grapes for winemaking.

Eudoxus of Cyzicus *(c.150 BC)*
At the western end of Alexander's former empire, fellow Greeks also continued to follow up on his early

explorations. As well as seeking out opportunities to investigate the Black Sea and northern European waters, individuals would work in the service of other nations if it meant the chance to venture even further afield. Eudoxus of Cyzicus was a key example of this principle. Although a Greek, his sponsors were the Egyptians. And although a European, his destination was, like that of Alexander, India.

Fifteen hundred years before Vasco da Gama, Eudoxus of Cyzicus undertook not one but two return sea voyages to the subcontinent. Unlike the Portuguese explorer, though, he did not need to round Africa to reach India. Working for Egyptian masters did have some advantages, not least a Red Sea coastline. It made an otherwise near-impossible journey more than realistic at a time when Eudoxus would have had few of the technological advantages in ship design or navigational aids that da Gama enjoyed.

For as long as mankind had been aware of precious stones, fragrant scents and fine spices, they had been desired, and men had been willing to risk their own lives or the lives of others in their pursuit. Egyptian Pharaohs were no different. Euergetes II (who reigned from 170–

163 and 145–116 BC) longed for the luxuries of kings. He decided Eudoxus would be his means of obtaining them, so the Greek was despatched with the ambitious aim of voyaging by sea to India to acquire this exotic cargo. What Eudoxus lacked in navigational tools he made up for in luck. At Aden, on the southern tip of the Arabian peninsula, he met an Indian pilot who had been abandoned in the city. Suddenly the prospect of a difficult journey into the unknown was considerably more straightforward. The pilot guided Eudoxus to his desired destination and the Greek obtained the cargo he was seeking.

Returning to Egypt with the hope of keeping at least some of his haul for himself, Eudoxus was to be quickly put in his place. The Pharaoh confiscated the entire contents of the expedition's vaults, from gems to spices to perfumes. By way of thanks, Eudoxus was dispatched to India again a few years later, this time to obtain goods for the new leader of Egypt, Cleopatra III (who reigned from 116–107 and 88–80 BC). Once more the Greek was successful, and once more he made vast profits. As before, though, the gain would be the Pharaoh's because the cargo made its way into his ruler's hands.

OPENING UP ASIA

Nevertheless, long before the modern era, the exploration of Asia and trade within it were clearly flourishing. From the eastern edges of Greece to the borders of China, early explorers and merchants had already mastered the lie of most of the land – and the seas – in between. The man who had mastered more than most, Alexander the Great, had helped blaze a trail in Asia which was actually thriving more than a thousand years before a new wave of explorers came again to 'open up' the continent.

Marco Polo *(1254–1324)*

'I have only told the half of what I saw', Marco Polo famously declared on his death bed. Yet even that fifty per cent was a fantastic account of eastern lands and peoples far beyond the experience of most European explorers up until that time.

In many ways, the fame that Marco Polo's name enjoys in history is a little unfair, for he was almost an 'accidental' explorer. If it had not been for the earlier travels of his father and uncle, Niccolo and Maffeo respectively, then the contacts that allowed Marco to undertake his extraordinary journeys through Asia would almost certainly not have been made. Furthermore, Marco only began his own travels as a teenager because his father had insisted on taking his son with him.

While Marco probably only had a minimal influence on his family's plan to travel overland to China, what distinguished him from Niccolo and Maffeo, in historical terms at least, was the fact that he made sure that his story was written down. Again, though, that was arguably somewhat of a coincidence. The man who became the author of Marco's travels, a writer named Rustichello, only wrote the story after spending a year in prison with Polo. The two men became cellmates when the Genoese captured them during a war with Marco's native Venice. During this confinement, Marco relayed the details of his earlier travels to Rustichello, who later released the best-selling book, *The Travels of Marco Polo*. It was partly because many did not believe its contents and partly because it was the most specific report of many of the cultures beyond Europe that existed on the continent at that time, that Marco Polo's name became legendary. Furthermore, the work became an inspiration to future generations of explorers, among them Henry the Navigator (*see* page 63) and Christopher Columbus (*see* page 105).

The overland journey Marco made from Venice into eastern Asia was immense but not unique. Since the rise of the Mongolian empire, which stretched from the borders of eastern Europe to China and the Pacific, ambassadors had been sent from the West to try to establish diplomatic relations with the Mongols. Earlier efforts had been made on behalf of the Pope by Giovanni da Pian del Carpini and, later, William of Rubrouck. Both emissaries made it through Persia and Central Asia as far as the Mongol capital of Karakorum, but without diplomatic success.

In the 1260s, however, Niccolo and Maffeo Polo, who were simply on a trading assignment in the Crimea, ended up being invited to travel to China by a Mongol ambassador. There they met the Mongol leader of China, Kublai Khan, and essentially by coincidence established the diplomatic breakthrough the Pope had been hoping for. They returned to Venice some years later with friendly greetings and gifts for the head of the Christian church.

So when, in 1271, Marco left with Niccolo and Maffeo on a return journey from Venice to what is now Beijing, he was not travelling into completely uncharted territory for a European. Nonetheless, the overland journey took them a gruelling three and a half years to complete. They passed through Asia Minor and Persia from where they had intended to take a sea passage to China. Unfortunately, they could not obtain a vessel that they felt would be strong enough to complete their long voyage, so they had to continue overland instead. Through Central Asia they trekked, crossing the harsh Gobi desert as they marched to their destination in China. The journey included a year of recuperation from an illness for Marco and also provided some vivid accounts in Marco's later book, yet even this epic undertaking was not the most extraordinary element of their time in Asia. Rather it was the fact that on arriving at the court of Kublai Khan, the Polos spent the best part of two decades in its service, exploring the far reaches of China and other areas of Asia in the process.

The Polos had a role in the empire's administration and helped prepare for its wars. At one point, Marco even became involved in collecting its taxes. Indeed, Marco, in particular, was favoured by Kublai Khan and represented his court on many far-reaching missions. His service took him to India, Sri Lanka, Burma, Southeast Asia, Siberia and Mongolia itself. In so doing, Marco was exposed to parts of Asia that, in some cases, Europeans would not see again for another five hundred years.

Marco was not only viewing 'new' terrain. When he later told his story, he recorded the details of the people and customs he had encountered on his epic journey, as well as tales of unheard-of inventions. These included the Chinese creation of gunpowder, printed books and, perhaps most ridiculous of all, paper money! He also told of an infrastructure of horses and messengers that had been established to rapidly carry the 'Imperial Post' across vast distances, allowing messages and letters to be sent through China with unbelievable speed.

In the process of their work and diplomatic representations, the Polo family accumulated a certain amount of riches for themselves. Eventually the problematic task of trying to safely transport this wealth back to Europe arose. After nearly twenty years in his service, the Polos persuaded Kublai Khan to allow them to leave for home, obtaining an imperial passport in the process to help ensure a return passage free from fear of robbery. As part of this deal, they agreed to escort a Mongol princess to an arranged marriage in Persia as their final duty to the Mongol court.

This time, the Polos opted to undertake the water route from China to Persia. Unfortunately it turned out to be no less treacherous or arduous than their outward voyage. The sea leg to Persia alone took nearly two years, only to find when they arrived that the princess's intended husband had already died! She was married to the deceased prince's son instead.

Once they had completed their duties, the Polos continued their return journey through Persia and Turkey and, finally on to Venice. They arrived in 1295, twenty-four years after they had departed, with a story so remarkable that it would endure to the present day.

Vasco da Gama *(c.1469–1524)*

Vasco da Gama is one of the most famous names in the history of exploration. He is celebrated as the man who completed the first sea voyage from Europe to India via the southern tip of Africa, opening up a new era in East–West trading relations. Yet he was also a notoriously merciless leader, resorting to sometimes horrific methods to achieve his goals, something that is often overlooked in the celebration of his achievements.

One of the main reasons for da Gama's selection as

the man to lead the expedition to India was this ruthless streak. Others had been sent on a route to the promised land that went past the Cape of Good Hope in Africa. They had often failed because of an inability to stand firm against the desire of their crews to return home. One such example was Bartholomew Diaz (*see* page 68) who had been the first to successfully round the Cape in 1487 but had been unable to force his men to proceed on to Asia. So King Manuel I of Portugal instead chose da Gama to complete the historic journey to India, believing he had the strength of character to fulfil his designated task.

The king was right. Da Gama stamped out any hint of mutiny in the early weeks of his voyage, which included an unusually long sea journey to southern Africa. Rather than follow the traditional route along the West African coastline, stopping along the way, da Gama felt that he could make better use of ocean currents and winds by taking a wide arc that initially headed westwards into the Atlantic as he headed south. It worked well, but it meant an uninterrupted three months at sea which tested the will of da Gama's men and the strength of his leadership.

Da Gama came through the trial, reaching the Cape

of Good Hope on 22 November 1497. Now followed the difficult journey up the East African coastline, hitherto unexplored by European sailors. By contrast, much of the coastline was well known to and, indeed, controlled by Arabic traders, who did not welcome the new arrival. In particular, da Gama encountered hostility from the Muslim merchants in Mozambique and the now Kenyan port of Mombasa. He was more successful further north in Malindi where the local ruler felt he could make a useful alliance against his competitor city Mombasa.

The good contacts made in Malindi also helped da Gama secure the knowledge required to make the final historic leg of his breakthrough journey. He obtained the services of a veteran guide to help him negotiate the ocean across to India. In less than a month, having taken advantage of the monsoon winds, da Gama landed at Calicut. The ground breaking sea-journey from Europe to Asia was complete.

Unfortunately for da Gama, the trade relations which would make this breakthrough so important did not follow anywhere nearly as swiftly. Da Gama's cargo had been loaded with a view to appealing to the less sophisticated trading stations along the African coastline, rather than the very prosperous ports of India. Consequently, da Gama had little of value to offer the Hindu ruler of Calicut and relations quickly soured. Furthermore, Arab traders also controlled this region and again were keen to drive out da Gama as soon as possible.

In some ways this lack of foresight regarding his Indian destination is surprising because King João II of Portugal had specifically sent out a secret spy operation to the subcontinent a decade earlier. Pero da Covilhão had been chosen to undertake the near-suicide mission, yet had succeeded in reaching India and despatching reports unveiling a wealth of new information.

Pero Da Covilhão *(c.1450–c.1524)*

The secret behind Covilhão's success had lain, of course, in the preparation. The plan was for the spy to reach Asia via the Red Sea. In order to arrive in India via this northern sea route, he would need to cross Islamic territory through Egypt, probably stopping in Aden in the process. The only way a Christian European could survive such a mission would be to disguise himself as a Muslim and for that he would need Arabic. No coincidence, then, that Covilhão had previously undertaken less ambitious spy duties elsewhere, including Fez in Morocco, where he learned the Arabic language. He also needed a new 'occupation', so as he journeyed through the Mediterranean to Rhodes he was reborn as an Arabic trader.

At this stage, Covilhão at least had a companion, another spy, Afonso de Paiva, with whom he travelled as far as Aden on the southern Arabian peninsula. While Covilhão's instructions were to head east from there, de Paiva's had been to head west into what is now Ethiopia (then known as Abyssinia) where the Portuguese believed the legendary (indeed, as was later realised, fictional) Christian King Prester John might be found, hopefully seeking an alliance.

In order to reach Aden, the two explorers spent more than a year crossing the Mediterranean and then travelling through Egypt, stopping in what is now Sudan, as they stealthily made their way along the Red Sea. In Aden, Covilhão found passage on an Arab boat that was making the journey across the Indian Ocean to the subcontinent. By 1489, he had successfully reached India. He visited both Calicut and Goa, all the time taking detailed notes of what he observed and the routes his party took, supposedly for the future benefit of his fellow

Portuguese adventurers. Certainly, India was the holy grail of trading promise that the Europeans had hoped it would be, with huge quantities of spices, perfumes, silk, gems, and gold changing hands. Yet in spite of this reconnaissance, Vasco da Gama had still subsequently travelled with unappealing trade goods.

Covilhão had nevertheless done his duty in attempting to ensure that his findings made it back to Portugal by succeeding in returning to the Arabian peninsula. He travelled along its coastline back to Aden and, towards the end of 1490, reached Cairo again. Here he met some emissaries who had been sent from Portugal to collect the notes Covilhão had made on his ground-breaking journey.

At the same time, Covilhão heard news of de Paiva's death, his mission unfulfilled. So, rather than head home, Covilhão simply journeyed to Ethiopia to complete his compatriot's unfinished business. En route, he even travelled through the Holy City of Mecca, the first European ever to visit the city that was forbidden to Christians. He would, however, be no more successful in finding the elusive Prester John, although he was welcomed by Emperor Eskender, ruler of the largely

Christian Abyssinia, who compelled him to remain in the kingdom for virtually the rest of his life.

In spite of all of this personal sacrifice and information-gathering on the part of Covilhão, though, little impact had been made on Vasco da Gama's own planning. Consequently, within three months of arriving in India, da Gama was forced to head home largely empty-handed. Worse still, he had been forced to take some hostages to negotiate the freedom of some of his own crew, who had been seized for failing to pay local taxes.

After a difficult thirteen-month journey home, three months longer than the voyage out, da Gama arrived back in Portugal with only two of his four ships and just fifty-four of his original crew of 170. Despite the heavy toll and his limited trading success, da Gama was welcomed as a hero for his historic feat.

In 1502, da Gama would set out on a repeat journey, this time with twenty heavily-armed ships. His mind was bent on revenging his ill-treatment at the hands of the Muslim traders and the Hindu ruler of Calicut. His anger was further fuelled by similar negative experiences encountered by his compatriot Pedro Alvares Cabral (*see* page 18) on a mission in the interim period. Da Gama's savage acts were many, including the bombardment of Calicut and the killing and dismembering of thirty-eight local fishermen as part of his terrorisation campaign to secure trading agreements. His most atrocious deed, though, was driven by a desire for vengeance against the hostility of many of the Muslims he had encountered. Consequently, he boarded and robbed a ship carrying nearly 400 pilgrims from Mecca. Once he had completed his plunder, he locked the hostages in the hold of the ship then set fire to it, resulting in the deaths of all of its innocent occupants.

In spite of this terror, da Gama himself only had limited success in setting up the trade agreements he was seeking with India. He had, however, opened the door for other missions. These would soon result in Portuguese dominance in the region and elsewhere in Asia. Often copying da Gama's ruthless displays of power and terrorisation, successive Portuguese explorers obtained the rich cargoes they desired. Faced with such might, many of the Asian ports that had been controlled by the Arab merchants soon signed trading agreements or were even colonised by Portugal, beginning the steady flow of goods by sea from the East to Europe.

Baron Nils Adolf Erik Nordenskjöld
(1832–1901)

The route from Europe to Asia via Africa remained rather cumbersome, though. For centuries, the European nations consequently continued to seek out the possibility of a sea passage around the north of the Eurasian land mass. If viable, the prize was potentially enormous: a shorter, more secure trade route to China and the rest of Asia, removing the existing need for the hazardous diversion around the southern tip of Africa.

Explorers were enthusiastic to take up the challenge, with many failing and some dying in the process. One early example was Willem Barents who, towards the end of the sixteenth century, made three attempts to find this elusive Northeast Passage through the sea that now bears his name. On the third journey his boat became trapped in pack ice and he eventually died of scurvy after a long winter out in the cold.

The man who did finally succeed where all others had failed was Nils Adolf Erik Nordenskjöld. His success came nearly three centuries after Barents had lost his life, by which stage thoughts of using this northerly route as a viable trading alternative had largely been abandoned due to vast swathes of ocean being frozen over for too much of the year. Nonetheless, Nordenskjöld's discovery and traversing of the Northeast Passage remains one of exploration's significant achievements.

Nordenskjöld was born a Finn but because of his political views he was exiled from his homeland by the Russian authorities in 1857. He settled instead in Sweden, where his family had ancestry, and it was here that he made many of the connections that would allow him to pursue scientific exploration for much of the remainder of his life.

The adoptive Swede persuaded his colleagues and sponsors that by undertaking the voyage in a steam vessel he could succeed in an attempt on the Northeast Passage where others had failed. In the past, efforts had largely been made in smaller, older ships that had become bogged down in the ice. Nordenskjöld thought that a larger steamship would not succumb to the same fate. He was not entirely correct, but nonetheless he would eventually succeed. Nordenskjöld's steamship *Vega* set out from Karlskrona on 22 June 1878 with a crew of twenty-one. Initially they made excellent progress and by September they were nearing the Bering Strait, the channel that separates Asia from Alaska.

This waterway was named for Vitus Jonassen Bering, who was credited with its discovery in 1728. Born in Denmark, but employed in the service of the Russian navy, Bering had been sent on a grand expedition to establish the north-eastern extent of Russia. In particular, he was ordered to confirm that the Asian and American continents were separated by sea and not joined together in one super landmass. This in turn would confirm the viability of an exit to any Northeast Passage around Russia and into China for possible trading purposes. Bering was successful in his mission, which meant that interest in completing the Passage would be sustained for generations to come. Unfortunately, he would not be the one to attempt the feat, having succumbed to disease in 1741 on what is now Bering Island, following an expedition to investigate Alaska.

So, a century and a half later, the challenge remained open for Nordenskjöld. As he made his way towards the Bering Strait, though, the Swede, in spite of his steamship and like so many before him, became locked in the ice. No further progress could be made that winter. The expedition would have to endure the long wait until the ice melted in the following summer before they could resume their journey.

Eventually, though, the team's patience was rewarded and in the following year they made it through the Bering Strait and on to China and the rest of Asia. Nordenskjöld completed his journey back to Europe via the more traditional route and returned home a hero. In 1880 he was made a baron in acknowledgement of his achievement.

Nordenskjöld's accomplishments were not limited to the Northeast Passage. Earlier in his career he managed to explore as far north as 81 degrees 42 minutes latitude. Indeed, he made a number of journeys to the northerly land of Spitsbergen and mapped it in the process. In 1872, he even contemplated an attempt on the North Pole, but had to abandon the expedition after his reindeer ran away! He also had a strong involvement in the exploration of Greenland. In 1870, he travelled further inland than anyone had ever previously managed. Later, in 1883, in the sea on the east side of Greenland he journeyed some seventy-five miles through its notorious great ice barrier, another first.

Furthermore, Nordenskjöld's achievements in exploration remained all the more significant because of his capabilities as a scientist and a cartographer. He left a vast legacy of books and maps that he had made during his northern expeditions, as well as an assembly of the works of others, which even today are considered to be invaluable. In 1902, shortly after his death, the entire collection was sold to the University of Helsinki, fulfilling Nordenskjöld's desire that the compilation should return to the land of his birth in one piece.

The completion of the Northeast Passage remained his finest accomplishment, however. By rounding the top of Asia, Nordenskiöld was concluding a process of exploring the continent's vast coastline that had begun literally thousands of years earlier. From Alexander the Great to Vasco da Gama and beyond, Asia had never disappointed: it was a constant source of exploratory wonder. Finally, though, the world was coming to understand the continent in its entirety.

Chapter 3

THE BIRTHPLACE OF HUMANITY:
Rediscovering Africa

Africa was probably the first inhabited continent on earth. With the exception of the polar regions, however, it was the last to give up its many secrets to explorers from the 'outside' world. What makes this more intriguing is that even from the time of the earliest records, Africa, or at least the more northerly areas, featured prominently.

Nonetheless, the majority of the continent would remain mysteriously hidden away from wider viewing until, in some areas, little more than a century ago. The 'New World' took less than five hundred years from discovery to complete revelation, yet until modern times Africa, which had been known to exist for millennia, stubbornly thwarted all who attempted to comprehend her.

Necho II *(c.600 BC)*

Known exploration of the continent actually began on a positive note. In around 600 BC, the Egyptian king, Necho II, sent out a fleet of Phoenician explorers, which is believed to have circumnavigated the continent. Originally from the Lebanon area, the Phoenicians had established trading posts and colonies across the Mediterranean region and were known at the time for their strength as traders and sailors.

Naturally, then, they were the perfect choice for Necho. He was a man for grand projects. The ruler had earlier attempted to build the equivalent of the present-day Suez canal that would link the Mediterranean to Arabia and Asia via a new water passage. It was an enormous project that was way ahead of its time and, although its failure was perhaps inevitable, the setback only spurred Necho on to try something that was arguably even more daring. He would send a fleet round an African continent that he only suspected could be circumnavigated. The Phoenicians he sent out not only proved this, but in the process completed a journey that both the Chinese and European superpowers of the fifteenth and sixteenth centuries would not manage for another two thousand years.

The reason that this achievement is perhaps not more widely hailed is because many doubt its authenticity. Knowledge of the journey is passed down through the Greek historian Herodotus in his *Histories*, and even he doubted the truth of some of the things that he recorded. Ironically, it was the specific point that Herodotus questioned which today leads historians to believe that the account is probably accurate.

The Phoenicians rounded Africa, or Libya as Herodotus then called it, in a clockwise direction, with the Egyptian Red Sea as their starting point. In the process, they would have entered the southern hemisphere. At this point, the sun's path would have been on the opposite side to what was 'normal' when sailing in any given direction. Herodotus would not have known the earth was a globe, so consequently he could not understand and therefore did not believe the Phoenicians when they reported this observation. He wrote:

> *These men made a statement which I do not myself believe, though others may, to the effect that as they sailed on a westerly course round the southern end of Libya, they had the sun on their right – to northward of them.*

Knowing today, by contrast, that the earth is indeed a sphere, the account becomes all the more believable. Only someone who had actually made the journey into the southern hemisphere at such an early time in history would be likely to be able to envisage such a story.

Even if we concede that this early report may be true, though, it does not mean that Africa became any more willing to give up her mysteries. Little else happened for the next thousand years, at least as far as the history of exploration is concerned. Finally, towards the end of the first millennium AD, the Chinese probably made it to East Africa. In the fourteenth century, the Moroccan Ibn

Battuta was among the first to record some of Saharan and eastern Africa's peculiarities, as part of his wider travels (*see* page 24). In the following century, Cheng Ho and the Chinese returned to survey even more of the African coastline, probably rounding the continent's southern tip for the first time since Necho's fleet (*see* page 27). And even though the Europeans also joined in the quest for knowledge from the fifteenth century onwards, inner Africa would continue to intrigue for another five hundred years.

If exploration was about bullying the lands and seas into surrendering their secrets, then clearly Africa was one continent that was not for pushing around.

Henry The Navigator *(1394–1460)*

Two thousand years after Necho II sent out a fleet to explore the African coastline, a Portuguese royal became interested in a very similar undertaking. His name was Henry the Navigator.

In many ways Henry had much in common with the Egyptian king. Both men are conveniently recorded as being great 'explorers' when neither of them actually took part in the expeditions with which they are credited.

Both, as leading statesmen, were interested in the trade and power that influence over Africa could offer. And both were responsible for overseeing breakthroughs in the history of exploration, forging a path for others to follow.

Above all, though, Henry's main contribution was his ability to organize wave after wave of sea voyages along the African west coast, long before any of the other European powers had even contemplated the idea. His primary interest was in seeing how far south along the African coastline he could encourage his ships and their pilots to explore, each time pushing that little bit further into the unknown. While he did not take part in the journeys, there is little doubt that his passionate promotion of them was the kick-start for a new golden era of exploration along the African coastline.

Although others would later ride the momentum he had set in motion in order to reach Asia, Henry's own aim was largely to spread the influence of Christianity into Africa. In particular, he wanted to outmanoeuvre the Muslim population in the north of the continent. Indeed, Henry had been part of a 1415 Portuguese military invasion of the Islamic town of Ceuta in Morocco. It is likely that this success encouraged him to aspire to track down what turned out to be the mythical kingdom of Prester John, a priest who was rumoured to rule a large Christian empire somewhere within Africa. An alliance with such a kingdom would have been attractive to Henry, creating the possibility of attacking the Muslims from the north and the south.

The invasion of Ceuta also opened up Henry's eyes to the wealth of luxury goods that arrived in North Africa on great land caravans from the east and the south, but which were denied to the Christian populations of Europe. He contemplated the possibility of bypassing this monopoly altogether by sea and carving out a Portuguese trading regime for himself and his country. The political strength such a move would bring, and the value of any alliances formed in the process, could also not be overlooked.

So, with the blessing of his father, King João I, he began establishing a systematic regime for the exploration of the western African coastline. He set up a base in Sagres on the extreme southwestern tip of both Portugal and Europe and brought together the ships, pilots, crews and navigators necessary to complete the mission he had targeted for himself. He possibly even took matters a stage further by establishing a naval academy and observatory at Sagres which would have researched, gathered and taught the knowledge and skills necessary for successful exploration en masse. In addition, a new type of ship, the caravel, was being built at around this time, which offered the perfect combination of operability, endurance and freight-carrying possibilities for long expeditions at sea.

However he managed it, there is little doubting the impetus that was given by Henry to European exploration in Africa. In the first fifteen years under his sponsorship, at least fifteen expeditions were sent out to explore. None of these managed to reach further south than Cape Bogador near the Canary Islands, because of a combination of difficult waters and the fear of the awful phenomena that, according to legend, lurked in the seas closer to the equator.

Gil Eannes *(Fifteenth century)*
In 1434, though, one of Henry's pilots, Gil Eannes, pushed on to the south of Cape Bogador on the journey that ensured his place in the history of exploration. He was a hero, yet a reluctant one, for Eannes's motivation

in succeeding where others had failed had primarily not been down to personal gain or national pride. Instead, he feared the wrath of Henry and the possible consequences that could befall him should he return to Portugal without having achieved his prescribed goal.

Eannes knew this only too well because just the previous year he had led an expedition that had failed. When he returned to Henry with the news, his patron at last lost patience at the continued failure of the expeditions, which could be put down to the fearful retreats of superstitious crews. So he turned Eannes and his ships round and sent them back again, with orders not to return without having conquered Cape Bogador!

The hard-line approach worked. Eannes overcame the trepidation of his men by steering a wide westerly course around the Cape, such that they did not see land again until they had already passed it. Clutching some 'Saint Mary's' roses, one of the few plants that could survive in the harsh climate on the coastline just beyond the Cape, as proof of his achievement, Eannes returned to Portugal as the pride of Henry's pilots.

With the physical and psychological barrier smashed at last, other expeditions were now free to continue further than ever along the western African coastline to places like Senegal, the Cape Verde islands and Guinea. Trading arrangements began to be established, although many of the early commercial 'successes' were based upon the capture and sale of slaves. Other hoards like seal hides and later gold also cemented the desire to keep on keeping on that Henry had instigated.

Consequently, by the time of his death in 1460, Henry's dedication and persistence had set in motion an appetite for Portuguese discovery that refused to stop with his demise. Although Henry's ships had only managed to reach as far south as Liberia in his own lifetime, waves of expeditions would continue until the African coastline had been conquered and viable trade routes to India and the Far East established.

Bartholomew Diaz (c.1450–1500)

The key event that opened the door to that goal was the rounding of the southern cape of Africa by Bartholomew Diaz, one of the many Portuguese explorers who continued to be sent out to charter the unknown after Henry's death. By the time Diaz's two fifty-ton ships, the *São Cristóvão* and *São Pantaleão*, left Portugal in August

1487, along with a supporting supply vessel, the African coastline as far as Namibia had by now been mapped, but the long hoped-for rounding of its anticipated southern tip remained stubbornly out of reach.

As Diaz reached the limits of previously charted waters a fierce storm descended, so he doubtless feared that it would remain beyond his grasp. The terrible weather lasted for two weeks, during which time Diaz's vessels were beyond normal control, being blown completely off course and away from sight of land.

Once the seas finally calmed, Diaz plotted an easterly course to try to make contact with the western African coastline again. This proved unsuccessful, so he switched to a northerly direction. This time he found land at Mossel Bay, on the other side of Africa's southern tip. The Portuguese had finally rounded the Cape and they had not even realised it or seen it! It was only as Diaz continued his journey further along the coastline towards Port Elizabeth and then the Great Fish River that he began to suspect his achievement, for the coast was running in an ongoing north-easterly direction. He contemplated sailing for India, but the crew were scared and the supplies were low, so he was persuaded to turn for home.

On the return voyage, Diaz sighted the elusive cape, confirming his achievement. He briefly named it 'Cabo Tormentoso' ('Cape of Storms'), after his eventful outward journey, but was overruled by the King of Portugal on his return. As the nephew of Henry the Navigator, João II had keenly continued to sponsor the spirit of exploration that his uncle had founded. Consequently, he recognised the symbolic achievement of Diaz's success and the optimistic trade prospects with India and the Far East that it opened up, so he renamed the tip 'Cabo de Bōa Esperança' ('Cape of Good Hope').

The Cape represented the end of one phase of African exploration and the start of a new one beyond. It was a psychological and physical milestone that, a quarter of a century after his death, was as much Henry the Navigator's achievement as that of Bartholomew Diaz. Not only Diaz but all those in the decades before him and the centuries afterwards were standing on the shoulders of the far-sighted vision of that one man.

Furthermore, while the Portuguese claimed nearly all of these early successes, Henry's determination and that of his pilots had also awoken the other major European powers to the trading and political possibilities in Africa and Asia (an awakening that would also result in the discovery of the 'New World'). It was the start of a 'golden era' of exploration.

René Caillié *(1799–1838)*

During the centuries immediately after the initial Portuguese successes, the exploration of Africa remained largely restricted to its coastal areas. The driving force behind European involvement in the continent was principally a commercial one. The maritime nations' demands were, for the most part, satisfied by small, secure trading posts and fortresses dotted along Africa's coastline.

In the late eighteenth and early nineteenth centuries, however, a new spirit began to take hold: exploration of the interior of Africa for the sake of exploration. This would later manifest itself in the European colonisation of the entire continent, but initially this was not the case. Africa was simply the ultimate jewel in the many treasures of exploration. Any adventurer worth their salt wanted a piece of this mystical continent. Whilst much of the world had already been discovered by this time, the interior of Africa remained stubbornly closed. It was the perfect adventure playground for any bold explorer game enough for the challenge. Few came bolder than René Caillié.

The Frenchman's stamping ground, like most of the early explorers of the interior of Africa, was the western side of the vast continent. Two mystical treasures in particular were sought. Firstly, there was the tracing of the course of the great River Niger, which was thought to weave its way through much of West Africa and possibly beyond. Secondly, and above all else, there was the uncovering of the shroud of mystery that surrounded the legendary city of Timbuktu. For centuries, rumours of this allegedly fabulously wealthy settlement on the southern edge of the Sahara Desert had pervaded: it was said that the streets and houses were literally drenched in gold. Yet it was so remote, being situated in a region that was hostile to Christians in particular, that no European had ever been able to penetrate the city in order to confirm or rebuke the rumours. This would be Caillié's achievement.

For all Caillié's success and new mapping of territory, though, he still had the benefit of the knowledge harvested from the four decades of other European expeditions in the West African interior that had preceded his achievement of 1828. In particular, this included the information gathered through the earlier adventures of Scotsman Mungo Park who, partially at least, had solved the first great West African question concerning the River Niger. Indeed, it was the bestseller, *Travels in the Interior Districts of Africa*, published by Park in the wake of his first expedition that, along with the tale of *Robinson Crusoe*, prompted much of Caillié's desire to take on West Africa in the first place.

Mungo Park *(1771–1806)*

Park, a doctor by trade, had been given his opportunity through the patronage of the 'Association for Promoting the Discovery of the Interior Parts of Africa', based in London, England. Formed in 1788, one of the society's key aims was to answer the River Niger question. No European had ever been able to travel its length or map its course. Indeed, there was even some doubt over the direction in which it flowed. Park was determined to be the man who found out for sure.

In 1795, Park received the Association's approval to map the Niger. An earlier adventure had been previously undertaken by Major Daniel Houghton who, before later dying in the Sahara desert, had suggested that the Niger ran in an easterly direction. Park's task, then, was to verify this theory and then journey along the length of the river until it reached the ocean.

After landing in the Gambia in June 1795 and spending a few months studying Arabic, he set off for the Niger in December. Very quickly, however, Park ran into trouble. Soon robbed of most of his possessions he was then captured and imprisoned by locals. One of his guides was sold and the other, Johnson, was left to endure confinement in the same appalling conditions as Park.

Four months later, Park escaped from his incarceration with the assistance of this guide. Rather than give up and return home, though, Park's determination was such that he pressed on in search of the Niger, even after Johnson refused to journey any further. With few possessions, little money and no guide, Park's subsequent arrival at the banks of the Niger in July 1796 was an incredible feat. Confirming Houghton's reports that it flowed in an easterly direction, he travelled along it for eighty miles, which took him beyond the town of Segu. His position being precarious at that point, he conceded defeat and returned home to report his findings.

Park was determined to complete the job, though, and in 1805 he secured, through the Association, another commission to find the Niger's mouth. This time he had the support of some thirty soldiers and ten other Europeans, including his brother-in-law Alexander Anderson and four boat-builders who would help construct the vessels required to take on the Niger. Local guides also assisted the party.

In spite of the much more substantial expeditionary force, though, Park's luck on arrival in Africa did not improve. Dysentery decimated the group and by the time they reached the famous river only eleven of the Europeans were still alive. A period of rest did nothing to improve matters and soon they were down to five, with Anderson also having succumbed.

Again, though, Park showed absolute determination in the face of adversity. Piecing together a boat from two canoes – nicknamed the HMS *Joliba* (the native word for the 'Niger') – he set off on his mission, accompanied by the surviving members of the party and some guides. In spite of everything, Park managed a thousand miles along the Niger before his luck finally ran out. At Bussa, his boat was attacked by natives who thought it carried raiders and his party had no option but to abandon ship for cover. The mystical river, which had been sought after for so long, now repaid the explorers' curiosity by drowning all but a single local guide.

So with much of the mystery surrounding the River Niger now resolved, although no-one still knew for sure where its mouth ultimately lay, René Caillié decided to focus his efforts on resolving the second great West African question: was the legend of Timbuktu actually true? What makes Caillié's achievements all the more remarkable is that he not only returned with the answers but, unlike Park, he did so without any backing from an expeditionary society or national government.

Indeed, Caillié was perhaps the most unlikely explorer that ever existed, for although he was forced to fund his adventures privately, he was no man of means. He was an ordinary, working-class Frenchman from the small town of Mauzé, whose father died in gaol and whose mother also passed away while René was still a boy. Yet despite poverty and the lack of any kind of social advantage, Caillié remained captivated by the idea of unveiling Timbuktu. At the age of only sixteen, and against all odds, he managed to secure for himself a berth on a ship to Senegal in West Africa.

It would take Caillié another twelve years, though,

before he could scrimp and save enough money to launch a serious attempt on Timbuktu. During this period he had been forced to return to France through illness and his employment had taken him to Guadaloupe in the French West Indies, but after every diversion he had eventually found his way back to Africa to try to achieve support for his mission. Each time, though, he failed. In 1825, finally giving up on any hope of French government backing, he made his way to the British settlement at Freetown to try to find support there. Again, Caillié was unsuccessful but he did at least find well-paid work as the supervisor of a British indigo farm. The appointment was not entirely coincidental, however, for the British themselves were in the process of launching an attempt on Timbuktu from the north, led by Major Gordon Laing. What better way to obstruct potential French competition than to distract it in Freetown with attractive employment?

Yet Caillié would have the last laugh. The work was so well paid that he was soon able to save up enough money to resign his employment and at last, in 1827, make his own private attempt on Timbuktu. The mere 2,000 francs with which he set out was still laughable by the standards and costs of most expeditions, but then

Caillié's approach would be very different from that of most expeditions.

Caillié had concluded that most European adventurers who had made any kind of attempt on West Africa's interior, including Park, had failed because they were just that: white, wealthy, Christian Europeans in an often poor, largely Muslim West Africa. They had stuck out like the proverbial sore thumb and were too tempting a target for robbery and murder, either on the grounds of their colour, riches, religion or nationality. Indeed, although Caillié and the rest of Europe did not yet know it, Major Laing had in fact managed to cross the Sahara and reach Timbuktu in 1826. As if to prove Caillié's point, though, he had been killed by suspicious natives on leaving the city, his journal and many of his reports being lost with him.

So, Caillié's solution was simple. He would travel as a poor, Muslim Egyptian seeking to return home after a childhood in the hands of the French, having been captured in Egypt by Napoleon's armies. His earlier preparation had been thorough, for it included a period of several months living in the desert with a group of Moors, learning Arabic and studying the Islamic faith.

It worked. For the best part of eighteen months, Caillié battled hostile terrain, weather, fevers, scurvy, poverty and those who questioned his story before he could ultimately reach Timbuktu and return to tell the tale. His route was far from direct: departing from Kakundi on the Rio Nunez in West Africa he was thereafter forced to join and travel with trade caravans on whichever routes they took, in order to avoid detection. Consequently his journey through West Africa often took him to areas that no white man had ever before visited. He made his way through Cambaya and Tiemé before finally securing a passage on the River Niger to Kabara which would bring him close to Timbuktu.

Here he disembarked and walked the few miles to the city of his childhood dreams, arriving on 20 April 1828. It was a disappointment, nothing like the legend – although it had once been a great trading town – and had declined to a series of mud huts in sandy streets, surrounding a central mosque. Nonetheless, he remained there for two weeks, studying the city and secretly writing notes on the pages of his Koran before departing.

Never one to do things the easy way, Caillié decided to journey home through the Sahara desert. The caravan he joined was nearly wiped out at one stage by lack of water but nevertheless he eventually made it to Tangier in Morocco. He revealed his true identity to the French Consul and was smuggled back to France where he ultimately received a hero's welcome. His belated rewards included a 10,000 franc prize from the Paris Geographical Society, the reimbursement of his expenses and a government pension. The English at first took some more convincing, refusing to believe a lone peasant had succeeded where the wealthily backed Major Laing had failed, but in time Caillié's achievements did become widely accepted.

John Hanning Speke *(1827–1864)*

With many of the mysteries of western Africa unravelled, European explorers now turned their attention to other outstanding matters in the interior of the continent. One fundamental question of African geography, above all others, remained unsolved: where was the source of the River Nile? Over thousands of years, many had unsuccessfully attempted to answer the conundrum. The Greeks had speculated on its source and the Romans had even sent an expedition to follow the river to its end, which became bogged down in marshland. By the mid-nineteenth century, still no-one knew for sure.

European hopes focused on the rumours of two vast lakes in the heart of Africa, one or both of which, if they existed, could prove to be the great river's source. The person whom history would credit with being the first to succeed in an expedition to validate this theory was Englishman John Hanning Speke. Yet, to all intents and purposes, this should not have been the case. The leader of the expedition that was to make Speke famous was his compatriot Richard (later Sir Richard) Francis Burton, to whom the glory should have been attributed. However, circumstance, illness and good old-fashioned sabotage intervened to present Speke with his chance. In grabbing it, accusation, vitriol and Speke's own mysterious death would follow, in a gripping drama fitting to the resolution of such a long-standing puzzle.

Sir Richard Francis Burton *(1821–1890)*

Before they set out for the great central lakes, Speke and Burton had worked together without any hint of the personal animosity that would follow. In 1854, Burton had led an expedition to explore modern Somalia and

Eastern Ethiopia. Speke, who up until that point had served in the British army in India, as Burton himself had done for the first decade of his own career, was invited to join the expedition. Initially it was successful. Burton, striking out on his own from the main party for a few months, disguised as a Muslim pilgrim, became the first Christian to enter the Holy Islamic 'forbidden' city of Härer. When he returned to the rest of the group at Berbera, though, the party's fortunes deteriorated. In April 1855, they were attacked by Somalis. One member of the group was killed, Speke was badly injured and Burton was thanked for his efforts with a spear through his jaw. They returned home in tatters to recover.

After the brief distraction of the Crimean war for both adventurers, Burton received the go-ahead to lead an expedition to answer the Nile question from the Royal Geographic Society in London and the Foreign Office. That Burton should have been chosen as its commander was only natural. He was the stereotypical heroic explorer and the British public loved him for it. An instinctive wanderer and a passionate investigator, Burton had striking good looks and no time at all for convention. He was nonetheless excellent at mapping his discoveries and was a brilliant linguist, fluent Arabic being among his many languages. It was this last skill in particular which had helped make him famous in 1853 when he had undertaken a daring voyage to the Holy Islamic cities of Mecca and Medina. As with his later trip to Härer, Burton travelled into the cities that were strictly off limits to infidels, on pain of death if discovered, disguised as a Muslim. Burton was also a prolific writer and translator, testing the bounds of Victorian perceptions of decency in the process by bringing the *Kama Sutra* to the British public, amongst other erotica.

Speke, by contrast, had none of the romance associated with Burton. Less cavalier, unwilling to travel in disguise or adopt his customs according to local habits, a poor linguist with little talent for accurately recording geographical and historical detail, and several years Burton's junior, Speke was in every respect the second-in-command when Burton received approval in 1856 to lead the expedition to the great lakes. Nevertheless, Burton had enough faith and respect in Speke's abilities, particularly as a hunter and as a stubbornly determined explorer, to personally select him as his deputy. They had evidently worked well enough together in the Somalia expedition in spite of, and perhaps because of, their very different personalities; with no indication of the controversy that would follow in the wake of this second African foray.

So it was that the two men set off from the African east coast port of Zanzibar in mid-1857, accompanied by a large party of guides, porters and animals carrying provisions and full of optimism that they would at last solve the Nile conundrum. Their target was to confirm the existence of what is now known as Lake Tanganyika, a huge mass of water that lay due west and which they hoped would prove to be the Nile's source. Almost immediately, though, the adventurers ran into difficulties, illness above all else hampering them. Consequently, it took them until February 1858 to reach the banks of Lake Tanganyika. By then, both men had suffered from malaria and Burton, in particular, continued to be afflicted by swollen legs which made it extremely difficult for him to press on. After learning from those who lived in the area that a large northward flowing river was not known to exit the lake, the men retreated to the Arabic trading settlement of Tabora to further convalesce.

It was here that Speke saw, and grabbed, his chance for

glory. By now the explorers had obtained news of the likely location of the second rumoured vast lake, thought to be due north of their new position. Burton, though, was too ill to continue. Speke, however, had recovered sufficiently to carry on and persuaded Burton to let him attempt to find the northern lake alone; indeed Burton helped him significantly in the planning of the route.

In contrast to their earlier travels, Speke's passage to Lake N'yanza, which he christened Lake Victoria, was a breeze. Within a little over three weeks he was standing on the southern banks of the vast body of water that he 'instinctively' felt was the source of the Nile. Burton captured Speke's thoughts on his discovery, after he had hurried back to Tabora to break the news:

> … he announced to me the startling fact that he had discovered the sources of the Nile. It was an inspiration perhaps: the moment he sighted the N'yanza he felt at once no doubt but that the 'lake at his feet gave birth to that interesting river which has been subject of so much speculation and the object of so many explorers.' The fortunate discoverer's conviction was strong; his reasons were weak …

Here began the controversy. Speke had not lingered long enough to prove his thoughts on what the discovery of Lake N'yanza represented. Burton continued to believe that Lake Tanganyika, or both lakes, or a combination of these and other lakes could still be the Nile's source: without full, scientific investigation they just did not know. Yet Speke was insistent and it began to create a split between the two men.

If this difference of opinion was the thin end of the wedge of division, then what followed next ruptured their companionship beyond reconciliation. Speke and Burton decided to return home to report their findings thus far. Yet Burton remained ill and, on reaching Zanzibar, could not complete the onward journey back to Britain. Again, Speke and Burton agreed to split up and once more the former manipulated the opportunity this presented. Speke set sail for home while Burton recovered in Africa, having made the gentlemen's agreement that they would wait until both were back in England before announcing the results of 'their' expedition.

The pact lasted barely as long as it took Speke to step off his ship on to dry land in May 1859. He not only made the results public but took the lion's share of the credit for 'discovering' both Lake N'yanza and Tanganyika. Furthermore, he made the unsubstantiated assertion that N'yanza was the source of the Nile. At that, Roderick Murchison, chairman of the Royal Geographical Society, furnished him with the backing to lead another expedition, without Burton, to prove as much. All this took place before Burton had even managed to make it home. It is small wonder that the two men became irreconcilably divided.

The harsh world of exploration had little room for sentiment, though, and Speke was thrilled to depart gloriously again for Africa in 1860. His plan was to head, with his new travelling companion James Grant, to the northern area of Lake N'yanza and hopefully discover a northward-flowing river. Anticipating that it would be the Nile, they would follow it until they met a prearranged rescue boat travelling up the river from Khartoum, which would take them home.

Once again, though, progress was slow. As well as illness, local wars and dogmatic rulers held them up this time, including the King of what is now Uganda, a mysterious country that hitherto no European had ever visited. Eventually, though, they made it to the northern end of N'yanza. In July 1862, Speke, who again had the good fortune to be travelling alone at that moment, because Grant was ill, stumbled across a northward-flowing river exiting the lake. He described his approach:

> *Here at last I stood on the brink of the Nile! Most beautiful was the scene, nothing could surpass it. It was the very perfection of the effect aimed at in a highly kept park; with a magnificent stream from six hundred to seven hundred yards wide ...*

He named the exit point Rippon Falls and began to follow the river northward as planned, to his rendezvous point at Gondokoro. Unfortunately, Speke's lack of scientific pedantry, and more difficulties caused by local tribal factors, meant that he did not always keep the river in sight as he took short cuts and alternative paths to his destination. This supplied his detractors back in England, the most vocal of which remained Burton, with sufficient ammunition to claim that he had still not proven N'yanza to be the Nile's source because he had not fully followed it from the lake to Gondokoro.

Here the drama reached its extraordinary conclusion.

After Speke had returned in triumph to Britain, a debate was arranged in September 1864 to try to settle once and for all the doubts which remained concerning his findings. Speke's main opponent at the debate would, of course, be the flamboyant and articulate Richard Burton.

The showdown never took place. The day before it was planned, Speke 'accidentally' shot himself in a hunting incident and died. Whether this was truly a coincidence or whether, because he feared facing the brilliant Burton in public, he took his own life, remains unknown.

David Livingstone *(1813–1873)*

The questions that Speke had left unanswered became one of the driving forces behind the continued expeditions of perhaps Africa's most famous explorer, David Livingstone. Yet, for all the motivation this gave him, Livingstone was by then already an accomplished adventurer in his own right, having started out in Africa when Speke was just a boy. He would also still be there long after Speke had entered his early grave.

Indeed, although Livingstone is perhaps best remembered for his efforts towards proving or disproving Speke's assertions on the source of the Nile, what was arguably his greatest accomplishment was under way before Speke had even set foot in Africa. This would be no less than to walk across the breadth of Africa, from one coast to the other.

Having dispatched his wife and children, who had hitherto lived and travelled with him in Africa, from Cape Town to the safety of Britain in April 1852, the missionary set out on an epic four-year journey. It was an expedition that would see the transformation of Livingstone from a preacher of God's word to an out-and-out explorer. Nevertheless, the spread of Christianity remained high among his priorities, but it was only one part of the solution to an issue that truly drove him: defeating the human slave trade. While he felt that 'civilisation' brought through the Bible could only help his cause, what would really undermine the slavers would be the opening up of Africa to legitimate trade and commercialisation. It was Livingstone's duty, therefore, to find the commercial 'highways' that would make Africa's interior available to merchants, and it was this search that saw him cross the continent.

Initially, Livingstone made his way from Cape Town across the familiar territory in which he had spent much of the last decade, in his then primary occupation of missionary. Indeed, it was this calling that had brought him to Africa in 1841, having been inspired by the London Missionary Society's representative in South Africa, Robert Moffat, to venture into the 'smoke of a thousand villages, where no missionary has ever been'. Previously, Livingstone, who had initially trained as a doctor after a poor childhood spent in Glaswegian cotton mills, had been intent on spreading the Word in China. A combination of the Opium War and Moffat's evocative lectures, however, persuaded Livingstone that Africa was his vocation.

So he made his way up to Moffat's home station of Kuruman, several hundred miles northeast of Cape Town. Livingstone gradually edged northwards, establishing new missionary stations as he went, eventually reaching Kolobeng, which was several hundred miles further inland on the eastern edge of the vast Kalahari Desert. During this period he also befriended and converted an influential tribal leader, Chief Sechele, an indicator of the empathy and humanity that Livingstone shared with native Africans: a skill that would prove to be the cornerstone of his success during his later forays.

It was to Kolobeng that he returned after sending his family home in 1852. From there he crossed the Kalahari Desert, an area he had previously explored with his wife during his quest for new mission stations, discovering Lake Ngami on its northern rim in the process. By 1853 Livingstone had reached Linyanti, from where he began to search in earnest for the commercial highways that he believed would be the panacea for Africa's ills. Shortly afterwards, Livingstone and a group of native assistants, loaned to him by another tribal chief he had befriended, Chief Sekeletu, encountered the banks of the Zambezi River at Sesheke. He was in the very heart of Africa from where he now aimed to reach the west coast in search of a viable trade route.

Heading northwest, initially alongside the Zambezi and eventually overland and away from the river, Livingstone endured a treacherous journey, ravaged by malaria and dysentery. Nevertheless, he successfully reached Luanda on the west coast in 1854. He took time out to recover, when he refused a passage on a British ship, not least because he felt obliged to guide his assistants back home: he then headed back from whence he came! The overland journey to Luanda had been so difficult that Livingstone realised that it could not represent the commercial highway he was looking for, so he made up his mind to return to Linyanti in order to look for a better route along the Zambezi to the east.

The return journey to Linyanti was no more pleasant, but again Livingstone endured, recovered and, with some more of Chief Sekeletu's men, set out again from the heart of Africa for the coast. It was during this period that Livingstone made some of the more romantic discoveries that have been associated with his name: above all the immense Victoria Falls, 'the smoke that thunders'. He continued along the Zambezi for most of the remainder of his journey east and successfully reached the coast near the mouth of the river in 1856. In so doing he had trekked over 4,000 miles across the breadth of Africa. Although the Zambezi did not prove to be the 'highway into the interior' he had hoped for, due to the impenetrable Kebrabasa Rapids that he had unknowingly skirted around on his journey east, Livingstone nevertheless returned to Britain a national hero for his remarkable feat.

While the Royal Geographical Society was sufficiently moved to award him a Gold Medal, its most prestigious honour, the London Missionary Society was less than impressed with Livingstone's move away from missionary-related activities into blatant exploration. Consequently, he severed his links with the Society and returned instead to East Africa in 1858, accompanied this time by his wife and brother, among others, to take up an appointment on behalf of the British government.

By contrast to his earlier successes, this period through to 1864 would prove to be one of a series of disappointments and setbacks. He discovered the Kebrabasa Rapids that blocked the route up the Zambezi, which he had previously missed. An inland missionary station within his domain, in the establishment of which his influence had played a large part, was decimated and quickly disintegrated. He was saddened to find that his one great discovery during this period, Lake Nyasa (now Lake Malawi) was a slave trading centre, and the boat that he built with his own money (almost his entire fortune), on which he planned to sail around the lake to try to discourage the slavers, could not be transported there and was not up to the job anyway. In the end, he was forced to take the boat to Bombay, where he sold it at a great loss. The money he did recover was placed in an

Indian bank which later failed, taking his assets with it! To top it all, Livingstone's wife and one of his sons died during this miserable period.

Many felt that one of the underlying reasons for Livingstone's struggles during these difficult years was the fact that he had the services of other European men at his disposal, the leadership of whom he had found difficult. Instead, he was at his best as a loner, the solitary white man working alongside a group of natives who trusted him and were guided by his instincts. Such was the premise of his last great, and probably most famous, journey into Africa between 1866 and 1873. The Royal Geographical Society wanted him to further investigate Speke and Burton's conflicting claims on the source of the Nile and look more closely into the series of great lakes they had uncovered. He had licence to conduct the exploration on his own and according to his own intuition.

After leaving Zanzibar, Livingstone made his way around Lake Nyasa over a period of several years, then up to Lake Tanganyika and from there to the Upper Congo, as he sought to clarify the Nile's source and the general geography of the region. He had to deal with all the usual hazards of illness, desertion, tribal frictions and malnourishment but, this time, the plunder of his relief supplies was added to the list. Among the goods he had ordered from the coast, which never made it, was medicine to counteract the ongoing debilitation of his health. By the time he returned to the shores of Lake Tanganyika at Ujiji in late 1871, the doctor's wellbeing was at its nadir: only to find, for a second time, that his relief medication had been stolen.

Henry Morton Stanley *(1841–1904)*

Enter Henry Morton Stanley. With a now famous 'Dr Livingstone, I presume', and a parcel of medicine, the outlook on Livingstone's expedition dramatically improved. Stanley had been sent by the *New York Herald* as a freelance reporter, to investigate what had happened to Livingstone. By now the doctor had been away for five years, and many thought him likely to be dead. If it had not been for Stanley's timely arrival, Livingstone probably would have died soon afterwards. Instead, his health recovered sufficiently to enable the two men to spend some time exploring the northern part of Lake Tanganyika and they became good friends during the brief time they spent together.

It was a period that would have a profound effect on

Stanley, because it enabled him to also become one of the great nineteenth century African explorers. Even before he had met Livingstone, his life story read like the most turbulent of dramas. Born as John Rowlands in Wales, he had passed much of a destitute childhood in orphanages or workhouses before escaping, on a ship as a cabin boy, to America in his late teens. Arriving in Louisiana, he gained employment with a cotton merchant who later adopted him. Such was his gratitude that Rowlands changed his name to that of his new patron, Henry Morgan Stanley. The American Civil War broke out in 1861 and, during the conflict, Stanley served in the army for both sides, spent some time in between as a prisoner of war and eventually ended up in the navy! After the war, he moved into journalism, covering a number of daring and glamorous assignments from rebellions in Europe to the opening of the Suez canal in Egypt to travels through Persia, before landing the Livingstone brief.

Having failed to persuade Livingstone to return to Britain in early 1872, Stanley's drama did not stop there. Journeying back to Zanzibar, and then to Britain, Stanley's account of his discovery of, and time with, Livingstone made him famous. It was an experience that had left him eager for more. By 1874, he had received the backing to lead another expedition from Zanzibar to map Lakes Tanganyika and Victoria. In the process he was able to accomplish what none of the others (Speke, Burton or Livingstone) had ultimately been able to achieve and that was to confirm for certain that Lake Victoria was the major source of the Nile.

As if that were not achievement enough, Stanley then solved another of Africa's great remaining questions, the path of the River Congo. Starting on the Lualaba River, to the west of Lake Tanganyika, Stanley followed its course until it flowed into the Congo, and from there followed the great river all the way to the Atlantic coast, becoming the first explorer to do so.

He returned to the Congo between 1879 and 1884, conducting investigations which would lead directly to the establishment of the Congo Free State. This in turn further turned the thoughts of Europe's squabbling nations to the ongoing colonial possibilities that Africa presented and intensified the general rush to grab land. Consequently, Stanley's last journey into Africa, beginning in 1887, the purpose of which was to relieve the stranded governor of a region in southern Sudan who had become isolated by rebel uprisings, represented perhaps the last great 'exploratory' expedition in a continent that was becoming increasingly familiar to Europe.

In spite of Stanley's later achievements, though, the romantic age of African exploration had arguably already ended more than a decade earlier with the death of the man who had personified the dream, David Livingstone. After Stanley had gone to the trouble of rescuing him, the Scottish doctor managed to live on for little more than a year after the two men had parted. Continuing his explorations beyond the southern end of Lake Tanganyika, Livingstone had become weaker, eventually dying in the heart of Africa in 1873. His two most loyal assistants, Susi and Chumah, would cut Livingstone's heart out and leave it in the soil of the continent, before embalming his body and carrying it to the coast for the long journey back to London.

Back in England, the identity of the body was confirmed by the sight of Livingstone's clawed left arm. It had famously been mauled some three decades earlier, fittingly by one of the few creatures that remained more dominant over the continent than Livingstone himself, a great African lion.

Chapter 4

VOYAGES TO THE NEW WORLD:
The Discovery of South America

While the Portuguese were busy working their way along the African coastline in an attempt to reach Asia, the Spanish at last woke up to the importance of pursuing a similar objective. They would approach the problem from a slightly different perspective, however. The Portuguese could have Africa to themselves.

Instead, with some persuasion, largely from a man named Christopher Columbus, the Spanish decided to try to reach the riches of the Far East by heading west. It was a revolutionary idea and one that would eventually pay huge dividends for the Spanish crown, although not in the way it initially expected.

No-one at that time had anticipated the rather large obstacle of the American continents and, as the Spanish would later discover, the Pacific Ocean, both of which blocked the way to Asia's great trade prizes. In Spain's particular case, the interruption would be the South and Central American mainland and the islands off its east coast.

As the realisation of what they had actually unearthed dawned on the Spanish powers, the disappointment of not finding Asia gave way to a determination to discover more about this new domain. In contrast to the Portuguese's lumbering (and ultimately largely incomplete) conquest of Africa, the Spanish took to the exploration game with a zeal rarely, if ever, seen since. Consequently, most of the truly great stories concerning the revelation of South and Central America come within only a few decades of Columbus's initial discovery, as the conquest of the continent was accomplished at an astonishing pace.

However, the events that form the basis of one extraordinary Latin American tale took place over two centuries later. As well as being an incredible feat in its own right, it also represents one of the earliest stories of exploration and adventure led by a female. Her name was Isabela Godin des Odonais.

Born in 1728, she was the daughter of the Spanish governor to Peru. When she was only in her early teens she was married to Jean Godin, a Frenchmen who had been posted to the region on a scientific expedition. A few years later, in 1749, he completed his work and was to return home by way of French Guiana on the northeast coast of South America. He decided to undertake the journey overland, by crossing the Andes and negotiating the length of the Amazon river. Wanting to take his family with him, but unwilling to expose them to the hazards of the journey without having ascertained its viability first, Godin set off from a point near Quito (in what is now Equador) without them.

He successfully arrived in Cayenne, French Guiana one year later. Confident of his route, his plan was to return to pick up his family, so that they could complete the same journey. Unfortunately, political tensions between the European powers in the region meant that neither Portugal nor Spain would grant Godin permission to undertake the expedition through their territories so that he could be reunited with his wife. Somehow, through misfortune, poor diplomacy and misunderstanding it took twenty years for Isabela's passage to be assured and news of the arrangement to reach her.

In 1769, leading a party of forty-two, Isabela finally set off on the epic journey to be reunited with her husband. As if enough misfortune had not already befallen her, however, the entire expedition was gradually wiped out through disease and accident, leaving Isabela as the only survivor. Starving and alone, her determination was such that she pushed on through dense jungle and hazardous waters. Somehow, and later aided by native Indians, she survived and eventually completed the remarkable 3,000 mile journey to Cayenne.

Reunited at last with her husband, the couple set sail a few years later for Europe, crossing the Atlantic in the opposite direction from the Spanish adventurers who had first opened up the continent more than two centuries earlier.

Christopher Columbus *(1451–1506)*

Christopher Columbus is often fondly remembered by history as the 'discoverer of the New World'. Yet, in truth, he neither discovered it nor realised that the land mass he had bumped into was indeed a vast 'new' continent. Firstly, it could perhaps be said with more accuracy that the Vikings had made the 'discovery' some five hundred years earlier (*see* Introduction to Chapter 5), albeit they landed in North America and Columbus the central and southern regions. On the second point, Columbus himself was responsible for undermining his actual achievements. He believed, and continued to insist, that he had not landed in a 'New World' at all but instead the eastern extreme of Asia.

In defence of the Columbus legend, however, he was in all practical terms the founder of an immense new world, at least to the dominant powers of Europe. The earlier forays of the Vikings had not been widely known about in the first place and any memories of their activities had been long since forgotten by the time of Columbus. Moreover, the fact that Columbus himself did not fully realise the extent of his 'discovery' did not, in the long run, really matter. There were plenty of others who soon did and within a few years they had fully grasped the magnitude of the opportunity for plunder and conquest that the Americas offered to Europe.

In fact, this is perhaps the most pertinent point when we consider what Christopher Columbus really achieved: by his determination to sail into the 'unknown' and return successful he awoke interest in the exploration of the New World in much the same way as Henry the Navigator and his successors did in the case of Africa and Asia. Columbus was the 'discoverer' of the Americas in the practical sense of the word, for he exposed its existence to a truly wider world, with all who followed thereafter basking in the luxury of being able to stand on his resolute shoulders.

Columbus certainly needed an unwavering determination just to see his ships lowered onto the seas in the first place. Almost every obstacle that could have been thrown in his way had been, as he battled to be taken seriously in his belief that he could reach Asia by sailing west rather than east.

Born in Genoa, Italy of a merchant's family, his background gave him little advantage when it came to climbing the social ladders that would allow him to embark on his later expeditions. He did, however, become acquainted with the ways of the sea at an early age, possibly starting out as a sailor when he was as young as fourteen. By his mid-twenties, Columbus found himself residing in Lisbon, Portugal after a vessel in which he was sailing was attacked and wrecked nearby. As Columbus progressed in his merchant career, the idea of an expedition to Asia by sailing west gradually gained momentum in his mind. By 1484, he had comprehensively formulated his plan for 'The Enterprise of the Indies', but there would be another eight years of struggle before he would finally find a sponsor to give him the go-ahead. It was a desperate period through which Columbus suffered derision, attempts to thieve his plan, rejection by the King of Portugal and, initially, rejection by the King and Queen of Spain after he sought patronage there from 1485. Eventually, though, persistence paid off and, in 1492, the Spanish royal court agreed to sponsor Columbus's grand plan.

In spite of all these difficulties, perhaps the biggest obstacles Columbus had to overcome were those that did not even exist at all! Myth and legend had held back Henry the Navigator's progress along the African coastline for years and similar superstitious behaviour had prevented any serious Atlantic exploration. Firstly, there was the fear of, quite literally, sailing off the edge of the world. Although it had been known that the world was in fact a sphere since the time of the ancient Greeks, many were still not aware of this fact or, if they were, they refused to believe it. Columbus knew it to be true, but all those who scoffed at the possibility of reaching Asia by sailing in the 'wrong' direction clearly did not. Then, of course, there were the usual fantasies of sea monsters and their ilk which perhaps induced an even greater fear. If this hysteria had been confined to the land-based masses, it would not have mattered too much but, unfortunately, it usually extended to ships' crews too. Columbus's men were no different.

Indeed, it was the crew that nearly stopped Columbus's first and most glorious expedition from succeeding. Having finally gathered his ships and sponsorship together and departed for the unknown in August 1492, Columbus's men were above all overcome by the very real fear of being out of sight of land for so long. This was not the case, however, for the early part of the voyage. Sensibly, Columbus had taken the precaution of heading for the Canary Islands after his departure from the small port of Palos in southern Spain. This allowed him to edge a few degrees westwards while still in the safety of known territory before launching head-on into the uncharted Atlantic. It also afforded him the chance to top up on fresh supplies and water and make repairs to the ships before beginning the truly epic part of their trip.

Pampered by this comfort blanket, then, the crews of Columbus's three ships, the *Santa Maria*, the *Niña* and the *Pinta*, did not voice too many concerns in the early stages of the voyage. As soon as they departed from the island of Gomera on 6 September and especially after they lost sight of the westernmost Canary Island, Hierro, on 8 September, though, matters began to change. Would they sail off the edge of the earth? What horrors of the deep awaited them? How could they trust their commander when he assured them that they would find land again?

Their fears grew stronger each day as they drifted endlessly westwards for more than a month without sight of land. Murmurs of discontent became voiced concerns and, as the days passed, the threat of mutiny was aired. In the end, Columbus was forced to do a deal with the men who wanted to turn for home. He assured them that if land was not sighted within a few more days, they would indeed retreat, although privately his journal indicated that he would stop for no man short of an overthrow of his leadership.

In the end, the threat evaporated anyway because on October 12 terra firma was sighted. Columbus had reached the Bahamas. There was land to the west! He named the first island upon which he disembarked San Salvador, then proceeded to investigate some of the nearby islands in the hope of finding the evidence to support his conviction that they had reached Asia. Within a couple of weeks Columbus had found his first substantial land mass in the form of Cuba and by early December he had also discovered the island of Hispaniola.

In between times, and at the height of his success, however, things had begun to go wrong for Columbus. As the overall commander of the expedition he was also in charge of its flagship, the *Santa Maria*. The other two vessels, the *Pinta* and the *Niña* were being captained respectively by two brothers, Martin Alonso Pinzón and Vicente Yáñez Pinzón. While the latter would be of significant assistance to Columbus later in their journey, Martin Pinzón was beginning to undermine his leader. On November 22 he had deserted his brother, and perhaps Columbus also, in search of gold on other islands. This in itself was a blow, but it became an even graver affair on December 24 when Columbus's own ship was wrecked off Hispaniola. This left only the *Niña* afloat and with the main party and it was too small to take all of the remaining crews home. Consequently, Columbus built a fort on Hispaniola which he called La Navidad and was forced to leave some forty of his men there with a promise to collect them at a later date. Meanwhile, Vicente Pinzón proved his worth by providing safe passage for Columbus himself on the *Niña*, in order that he could return to Spain and reveal their findings.

Coincidentally, Columbus did in fact bump into Martin Pinzón on his way home. The two ships were reunited and strong words were exchanged, but not long afterwards a storm separated them again. They both therefore raced for home alone and although Martin Pinzón made it back to the European mainland first, possibly in the hope of stealing some of Columbus's glory, Columbus actually beat him back to their home port of Palos by just a few hours, on March 15 1493.

Columbus was a hero. All those who had doubted him

had been proven wrong and he had brought glory and success to his Spanish sponsors. At his zenith, it would perhaps have been fortuitous for his historical profile if he had done what Martin Pinzón did at this juncture and promptly died. For as if Pinzón's own behaviour and the sinking of the *Santa Maria* had been a forewarning of bad luck to come, things pretty much went progressively downhill for Columbus after this point.

Columbus went on to undertake three further expeditions to central and southern America, still refusing to believe that he was not in Asia. In spite of the continued discovery of new land, he struggled to live up to his earlier achievements. The main purpose of his second expedition, between 1493 and 1496, was to try to find the Asian mainland. Given that he was still a continent and an ocean away from it, though, it is not hard to believe that he would be disappointed: he not only failed to reach Asia but also the American mainland. Furthermore, he had made good on his promise to return to La Navidad, only to find that his men had been massacred by natives.

The second expedition, therefore, was mostly taken up by sailing among many of the same islands that Columbus had already discovered. To be fair, he did also manage to reach Jamaica, as well as establish a new colony at La Isabela on Hispaniola. In addition, Juan de la Cosa, the former owner of the *Santa Maria*, sailed with Columbus on this trip. His experiences with Columbus, along with a later voyage under Alonso de Ojeda (who was also on Columbus's second expedition), contributed to his ability to draw what is now the oldest surviving map of the 'New World' in around 1500.

Columbus's third voyage took place between 1498 and 1500. Again, he should probably have stayed at home, not least to improve his continually ailing health. At least this time, though, he briefly made it to a point on the South American mainland that is now Venezuela, but equally he also made it to the inside of a prison cell. The sequence of events was that after splitting his six-ship fleet in two and sighting Trinidad as well as the mainland, Columbus returned to the other half of his party, which had been engaged in taking supplies to colonists at Hispaniola. By now, a new city called Santo Domingo had been established and the colonists there were in revolt against Columbus's handling of the island's affairs. Although he managed to calm matters on his arrival, the King and Queen of Spain were also beginning to lose faith in their man. They decided to send out Francisco de Bobadilla as the new royal commissioner to the colony. His first action on arriving on the island was to arrest Columbus for mismanagement and send him home in chains. The great explorer's humiliation was complete.

Columbus did manage to salvage enough of his reputation on returning to Spain to win his freedom. He even persuaded his rulers of the merit of a fourth expedition between 1502 and 1504, but he never really recovered from his earlier treatment. There were some successes on this voyage, however. Columbus investigated a reasonable stretch of central American coastline from Honduras down to Panama, encountering natives who possessed large quantities of gold in the process. Again, though, all this came at a price. The fort he built in Panama was attacked by locals with the loss of several men. In his rush to abandon the settlement, Columbus had to leave one of his four ships behind. Over the next few weeks, his remaining vessels succumbed to either shipworm or storm damage and they too were wrecked, with the entire party becoming stranded in Jamaica. One of the party kayaked to Hispaniola to obtain help, where he was unsympathetically arrested. Many of those remaining with Columbus tried to mutiny in the year before their eventual rescue.

Columbus returned to Spain, his reputation still much diminished from its earlier peak. He died within a couple of years, stubbornly clinging to the mistaken belief that he had reached Asia. He felt that his last voyage had confirmed this when, on talking to natives in Panama, he learned that there was another great ocean on the nearby southern coast of the land mass. They were, of course, referring to the Pacific. Columbus, though, believed that this would be the Indian ocean, in which case the already recorded Strait of Malacca (actually near Malaysia!) would doubtless soon be found in the vicinity and the much desired short cut to Asia revealed.

He was so desperate to be remembered for this oriental achievement that he remained ignorant of his much grander accomplishment – bringing the Americas to the world – until his dying day.

Amerigo Vespucci *(1451–1512)*
If Christopher Columbus 'discovered' the 'New World', then why is the world's most powerful country not called the USC ('United States of Columbia')? Why instead

was the name *America* taken from that of the Florentine explorer *Amerigo* Vespucci, a man who clearly arrived in the New World after Columbus?

These questions have aroused such passion over subsequent centuries that Ralph Waldo Emerson's 1856 statement on the matter, 'Strange that broad America must wear the name of a thief', was not untypical. Yet it seems likely that Vespucci himself played little if any part in the controversy which surrounded the naming of a nation after him.

It is perhaps a little ironic, then, that neither Columbus nor Vespucci actually set foot on what is now mainland USA. They both did, of course, make it to the Americas, albeit their mainland excursions confined them entirely to the central and southern American continent. In Vespucci's case, even the number of expeditions he undertook to these areas is in historical dispute, with different documentary accounts putting the number at either two, three or four between the years 1497 and 1504.

With such controversy surrounding the man, then, it is perhaps best to focus on his many 'known' facts and achievements. His first 'certain' voyage took place from May 1499 to June 1500 on behalf of the Spanish throne.

By this stage Columbus was already on his third voyage to the region. Like the great man himself, Vespucci similarly believed that Columbus had discovered the other side of Asia. Consequently, he set sail under the overall command of Alonso de Ojeda with the intention of succeeding in finding a passage through to 'known' Asia where Columbus had so far failed.

The captain of the overall mission, de Ojeda, now tends to be overlooked by history in favour of Columbus and Vespucci, but he too was a determined and experienced man in his own right. He had taken part in Columbus's second expedition and it was this new expedition, which included Vespucci, that also enabled Juan de la Cosa to gather many of the remaining details for his famous map of the New World. Furthermore, de Ojeda would sail along a significant portion of the northeast coastline of South America, the first outsider to see much of this territory. He also soon established for himself a reputation for brutality, particularly in his encounters with the American natives. In later attempting to establish colonies, he would exercise extreme cruelty against the locals, taking slaves as he pleased. In one attack designed to avenge the death of de la Cosa and many of his men, who had been ambushed by natives at the short-lived colonial settlement of Cartagena in Colombia in 1508, de Ojeda destroyed an entire village of one hundred houses. He killed all of its inhabitants, men and women alike, save six children.

For all de Ojeda's ruthless determination, though, Vespucci was just as focused on achieving his own goals, if in a less heavy-handed fashion. Once across the Atlantic in 1499, Vespucci split his ships off from de Ojeda and headed south, probably becoming the first European to see the mouths of the Amazon river and what is now Brazil.

Indeed, as with much of the detail that surrounds Vespucci's accomplishments, the identity of the true 'discoverer' of Brazil is still open to some debate. History books often record Pedro Álvares Cabral as the country's founder yet, at best, he was probably only the leader of the third European party to land there. The reason he is generally recorded as the earliest outsider, though, is because he was the first Portuguese explorer to arrive. Significantly, in terms of the future cultural and lingual development of Brazil, Cabral claimed the land for Portugal when his fleet landed there in April

1500. The Portuguese and the Spanish had a prior agreement, adjudicated through the Pope, giving the Portuguese exclusive title to new lands discovered to the east of an imaginary demarcation line (drawn 370 leagues west of the Cape Verde Islands) which lands significantly included Africa. The Spanish, meanwhile, had first claim on anything to the west, including most of South America. Part of Brazil, however, jutted into the Portuguese domain and it was through this device that Cabral was able to whip away the new land from under the noses of the Spanish. Thus were the beginnings of Portuguese influence in Brazil and, as such, why Cabral is often remembered as its founder.

The Spanish had more than a little reason to feel miffed. Firstly, Cabral was not even supposed to be sailing for Brazil. Instead he was leading the second Portuguese expedition to India. On attempting to round Africa, it is thought that he accidentally sailed too far west and bumped into Brazil in the process (some have even suggested that this was actually a deliberate ploy to steal the land away from the Spanish, but the generally accepted story remains that it was an accidental discovery). It would turn out to be a hugely significant expedition for Portugal and the countries that came under her sphere of influence as a result. Not only did Cabral take Brazil but, en route to Asia, he claimed what became the Portuguese colonies of Mozambique and Madagascar and firmly established Portuguese influence on the southwestern ports of India.

Secondly, and more importantly, though, the Spanish were convinced that they had arrived in Brazil before Cabral. Certainly, Vicente Yáñez Pinzón, who had performed so admirably as commander of the *Niña* on Columbus's first voyage, had set out on an expedition to the area in 1499. He arrived at Brazil in January 1500 and then spent many of the next few months surveying its coastline, including the mouths of the Amazon. Thus, he is also regarded by some as the 'discoverer' of the country (although, there are other reports that he was merely following up an earlier unrecorded visit to the region by his now deceased brother Martin Pinzón).

Then, of course, there was Vespucci, who probably trumped them all in the timing of his arrival in Brazil, yet he is less remembered for this than for his other achievements. If his own reports are to be believed he beat Pinzón there by several months and was the first to see many of the landmarks, including the Amazon, with which Pinzón is often credited.

What is certain is that the 1499 to 1500 expedition was a very successful one for Vespucci and it did much to establish his reputation. After he returned to Spain from this triumphant foray he began making plans to head even further south on another expedition that would find and round the southern tip of what he still believed to be East Asia.

So it was that he set sail again in May 1501, this time funded by Portuguese sponsorship with a fleet entirely under his own command. Once he reached the Brazilian coastline he headed south for thousands of previously uncharted miles, past present-day Uruguay and along Argentina. It was at this point that Vespucci made the mental shift that distinguished him from Columbus. His journey alongside this epic land mass made him realise that he was not looking at Asia, in fact, but a new continent altogether.

This conclusion was reinforced by the significant breakthrough he had made on his travels: he had devised a much more accurate method of calculating longitude than had ever previously existed. It enabled him to develop a prediction of the equatorial circumference of the earth, which was later proven to be only fifty miles short, and to anticipate that another great ocean on the other side of the 'New World' would intervene before Asia was encountered.

In the end, when Vespucci turned around he was only 400 miles away from the southern tip of South America, but by then he had seen enough to come to his most important conclusions. He arrived back in Lisbon in July 1502.

Despite his correct belief that he had indeed been looking at a new continent, it was not even at this point that Vespucci made any obvious attempt to have the Americas named after him. That historical quirk was, it seems down to a German scholar and cartographer by the name of Martin Waldseemuller.

In 1507, Waldseemuller produced a pamphlet called *Cosmographiae introductio* followed by an updated map of the known globe in which he suggested that the 'New World' that Vespucci had advocated should be named after the man. Furthermore, it was believed at the time that Vespucci might have made an earlier voyage across the Atlantic in 1497 which, if true, would have had him reaching the American continental mainland before Columbus (who up until that point had only seen the islands off the mainland) and even John Cabot (*see* page 147). Although this voyage is not now believed to have taken place, Waldseemuller was none the wiser at the time and he therefore lobbied to have the New World named in Vespucci's honour. From a Latin derivation of Vespucci's forename, he labelled his map of the southern continent 'America'. In 1538, Gerardus Mercator's famous map extended this label to the northern continent as well and so the name was cemented in history. Although Waldseemuller later realized that his choice of name might not have been the fairest, the word *America* was already being used too widely to withdraw it. Columbus had missed his place in the New World sun.

Vasco Nuñez de Balboa *(1475–1519)*

While Vespucci's naming of the New World continents might have been more accidental than premeditated, the actions of many more players in the early exploration of South and Central America were far more opportunistic. Indeed, after the initial discoveries to the west, Latin America soon became an adventure playground for almost any Spanish 'conquistador' who fancied a little glamour and danger as a distraction from life back home. There were few greater chancers than Vasco Nuñez de Balboa. His life, achievements and, ultimately, demise were all defined by his unceasing speculation in 'Spain's' new domain.

Balboa's two decades of adventure began when he left his Spanish homeland in his mid-twenties on an expedition organised by Rodrigo de Bastidas in 1500. Although born into the lower nobility, Balboa was not from a wealthy family and up until this point had worked in the service of more affluent aristocratic masters. Being based near the Atlantic coast at Moguer, however, Balboa had been exposed to tales of the New World from the mouths of the sailors and explorers who had been there, and, more importantly, had learned of the wealth and opportunity it offered.

Initially, though, it proved to be a disappointment. Bastidas's expedition undertook some exploration along the northern coastline of what is now Colombia, but it had insufficient supplies and resources to establish any kind of settlement there. So, instead, they retreated to the already well-established colony of Hispaniola. Here,

Balboa decided to set himself up as a pig farmer. He was spectacularly unsuccessful and was soon worse off than he had been back home in Spain.

Indeed, so bad was Balboa at his new job that he became deeply in debt. Again, escape to a new life became his only real hope of salvation, but even that door was now closed to him because his creditors thwarted his attempts to leave the island while he still owed them money. Consequently, Balboa threw in his lot with serendipity again. Unable to depart Hispaniola legitimately, he stowed away on a boat belonging to the 1510 expedition of Martin Fernández de Enciso. Had Balboa been less fortunate, or less of a quick-talker, he could just as easily have found himself thrown overboard when he had made his presence known once the ship was safely out to sea. But his charm persisted and Enciso agreed he could stay, even help guide the expedition along some of the mainland coastline that Balboa had previously visited with Bastidas.

The party's initial aim had been to bring relief supplies to San Sebastian, a newly founded and short-lived settlement on the South American mainland. The expedition was to discover, though, that many of the inhabitants of the colony had been massacred by local

Indians and, by the time of Enciso's arrival, it had been abandoned altogether. Again, Balboa saw an opportunity in adversity and stepped up to the fore. He persuaded Enciso that he had previously encountered more peaceful Indians to the west and, by making use of his supplies, a new town could instead be established there. So the settlement of Santa Maria de la Antigua del Darien was born, and it became the first successful colony the Spanish had managed to establish on the mainland.

Not content with escape from his creditors to settle for another shot at the quiet life, Balboa soon became embroiled in the new town's politics. His relationship with Enciso turned sour and, through stealth, charisma and a greater affinity with the majority of its inhabitants, Balboa effectively became the unofficial leader of Darien. When Diego de Nicuesa was sent by the Spanish king as the town's new governor in an attempt to try to stabilise the infighting, Balboa usurped him as well, at risk of being impeached for treason.

Having triumphed over Enciso and Nicuesa, but realising the danger such disobedience, effectively of the Spanish crown, could bring, Balboa again resorted to opportunism to save his skin. Once more, fortune favoured the brave. The activities he undertook at this juncture would immortalise him as an explorer and are the principal reason that he is remembered today.

Balboa realised that he needed to carry out some kind of grand action to bring him back into favour with the Spanish royal family. Few would argue that this was exactly what he achieved next. The 'discovery' of the Pacific ocean, even on the extensive scale of world exploration, is up there with the grandest of actions.

While Balboa had, at times, been fairly ruthless in his quashing of certain Indian tribes in his settlement of Darien, including the use of horrific torture techniques, he was not systematically brutal. Being the canny political opportunist that he had already proven himself to be, he also realised the benefit of befriending other tribes when it suited him. It was his good relations with several of these tribes that brought him the news that there was a vast sea only a few days march away, on the other side of what is now the isthmus of Panama. Balboa wanted to investigate for himself, and again his Indian friends came to his aid, providing guides and advice on the most appropriate route.

In early September 1513, Balboa set sail for Acla which lay at a narrower part of the isthmus, before beginning his overland journey to the southern coast from there. On the way, he both encountered more friendly tribes who confirmed the existence of the great body of water that Balboa sought and suppressed others who tried to stand in his way. Among the two hundred or so Spaniards that Balboa had taken with him to ensure his safe passage was his ruthless lieutenant, Francisco Pizarro, who would later make his own name as a conquistador through his destruction of the Inca civilisation in Peru. Indeed, it is highly possible that the Indians who befriended Balboa also relayed rumours of the wealthy and sophisticated Inca society, which perhaps planted the initial seed in Pizarro's mind.

Before the end of the month, Balboa had ascended the last mountain peak that stood between him and the Pacific ocean. Early European traders might potentially have viewed the great expanse of water from its western end, but Balboa was certainly the first European to see it from its eastern rim and he is generally credited with its 'discovery'. Within a few more days he was wading into the water itself in full armour, his sword and his country's flag held aloft, claiming the ocean and all the lands that it bordered for the King of Spain. Messengers were dispatched back to the fatherland with news of the find and King Ferdinand was suitably pleased. The discovery had done the job and Balboa was let off the hook for his earlier insubordinate behaviour. Moreover, it brought in return a new title, 'Governor of the *Mar del Sur* (or 'South Sea', as Balboa had initially named the ocean), Panamá and Coiba'.

It was only a temporary reprieve, however, and it was at this point that the chancer's luck finally ran out. While the news of his discovery had been welcomed with the conferring of Balboa's new title, it had arrived too late to prevent the dispatch of Pedrarias Dávila as the new overall leader of the territory in which Balboa operated. Pedrarias had been appointed Governor of the Crown Colony of Castilla del Oro, the newly renamed and now officially recognised title for Darien. In spite of Balboa's own appointment, he was still to report directly to Pedrarias. The two men did not see eye-to-eye in the slightest, and this time Balboa would not be the victor in the ensuing power struggle.

Pedrarias, a jealous and bitter man by nature who felt even more threatened in the presence of a rival who could claim the achievements of Balboa, did everything within his power to thwart any further exploratory successes by his subordinate. In return, Balboa did everything he could to undermine Pedrarias's authority in an attempt to expose him as unfit to govern. In spite of this hostile climate, Balboa was successful in building and transporting a fleet of ships to the Pacific coast in order to facilitate further exploration of the new perimeter, although the expedition itself achieved little in the limited time Balboa had left.

Indeed, Balboa was arrested and brought to trial on trumped up charges of high treason by his nemesis Pedrarias. So convincing had Balboa been in his efforts to undermine his governor that the King of Spain had announced his intention of replacing Pedrarias and conducting a full investigation into allegations of incompetence and mismanagement of the colony. Realizing the damage Balboa and his supporters would cause to his reputation during any questioning, Pedrarias hastily arranged the treason trial and ensured that his rival was convicted before the assessors arrived. Consequently, Balboa and four of his colleagues were beheaded at Acla in January 1519. The man who had spent his life on the run had finally run out of places to hide.

Hernán Cortés *(1485–1547)*

Just as Balboa's luck was disappearing along with his head, another conquistador decided that it was time to try his. His focus was Mexico, which was further to the north than Balboa's former domain. In most other respects, however, their approaches were identical. The new man's name was Hernán Cortés. Like Balboa, Cortés would gamble everything on the attainment of glory and New World riches. He calculated that he could similarly disobey orders and escape punishment as long as he delivered a sufficient prize into the hands of the Spanish realm. On achievement of his goal, the conquest of the great Aztec empire, he was proved correct.

Although Balboa and Cortés had much in common, the latter was probably a slightly more rational gambler. He literally managed to keep his head when Balboa did not, and this difference of outcome is perhaps not entirely coincidental. He was more politically astute and more premeditated in his risk-taking. Accompanying his undisputed courage was a certainty of purpose in decision-making. He inspired the men who fought for him and displayed all the qualities of a truly great leader, which probably goes some way towards explaining how he conquered the strongest empire in Central America with a force that initially comprised little more than 500 men.

The early life of Cortés does not appear to have predestined his later exploits. Although of noble parentage, Cortés's family was not wealthy. He had been a lousy scholar and had shown no aptitude for the career in law for which he was supposed to have been groomed. He did, however, love reading and hearing the stories of adventurers in the New World. So it was no surprise that by the age of only nineteen he was already on a ship to Hispaniola. As with Balboa, his early years in the thriving Spanish colony were unremarkable; he farmed and he trained as a soldier.

By 1511, though, Cortés was ready for new adventures so he signed up for his first conquest. Diego Velásquez was at that time leading an expedition to fully subdue and settle neighbouring Cuba and Cortés was keen to join him. He served his master well during the successful mission and the prestige of both men grew in its wake. Velásquez became Governor of Cuba and Cortés soon attained the position of mayor of the colony's capital, Santiago.

It was Cortés's first real taste of politics and leadership and he thrived in his new environment. So too did the colony as a whole, such that within a few years the Spanish were again looking for more territory into which to expand their successful settlers. The American mainland was the obvious answer. Balboa was already busy at work further south but Velásquez had his eye on what is now Mexico, only a short hop west from Cuba. Between 1516 and 1518, he sent over a couple of exploratory expeditions and, as well as reports on the lie of the land, Velásquez's men returned with rumours of a rich native empire to the north.

By 1519, Velásquez was ready to find out more about what would turn out to be the Aztec civilisation so that he could explore some of their territory and begin trading with them in an attempt to exploit their wealth. The man he decided he could trust to lead such an expedition was Hernán Cortés. Or at least he thought he could at first. No sooner had Cortés come close to completing his preparations than the Governor of Cuba changed his mind. He suspected that Cortés might be developing ambitions for the mission beyond his remit and, worse, might seek to claim any glory for himself.

He was right. But he was also too slow. On hearing Velásquez's order for him to step down from the project's leadership, Cortés simply ignored him. He sped up his final preparations and hastily departed with his 500 or so men, sixteen horses and some pieces of artillery. Hardly a force with which to completely conquer the region's strongest empire, but that, in further disregard for Velásquez's wishes, is exactly what Cortés had decided to do.

Within a short time he had reached the mainland. Cortés marked his intention to stay by founding the city of Villa Rica de la Vera Cruz as his base, and then destroying the fleet of ships upon which they had arrived! Some of the men had been questioning the wisdom of embarking on a major conquest with such a small force, so to quell any threat of mutiny Cortés had taken this drastic action. They would either succeed or die trying, their leader told them. It was a gamble, but as with his decision to defy orders in the first place, a calculated one. It seemed to work. Left with little alternative, the force was energised into action by Cortés's confidence and so they set off for the interior. Their target was the beautiful Aztec capital of Tenochtitlán.

The Aztec empire had itself only been carved out during the previous couple of centuries and it still had many enemies amongst the tribes and lands it had conquered. Consequently, Cortés found it relatively easy to convince many of the dissenting natives to join him in his march on the capital. In true conquistador style, he fell in love with a native girl known as Malinche along the way. She became his interpreter and guide, further helping his cause in obtaining new allies.

Not that Cortés had any need to worry, at least not in the beginning anyway. On his arrival in Tenochtitlán, the Aztec emperor Moctezuma instructed his people to greet him warmly and like a god. Aztec legend had long predicted the return of the white-skinned deity Quetzlcoatl and, to his good fortune, Cortés's complexion fitted the bill perfectly.

The goodwill did not last long, however, and soon Cortés was grateful for the extra allies he had recruited along the way. In a move designed to deflect attention away from reports reaching Tenochtitlán that some of Cortés's forces had been killed by natives back in Vera Cruz, thereby exposing them as mere mortals after all, Cortés rather riskily kidnapped Moctezuma. The huge ransom in gold that he demanded for the emperor's release was paid, but he continued to keep the Aztec ruler locked up anyway.

As if these events were not trial enough for Cortés, Velásquez chose this moment to send a force to rein in his errant subordinate. Cortés was compelled to divide his already tiny force between the capital and a party sent to do battle with the incoming Spaniards. Remarkably, Cortés not only succeeded in defeating his would-be captors but he convinced the remnants of the surrendered Spanish army to change sides and join him.

More trouble awaited Cortés back at Tenochtitlán, though. The unprovoked massacre of certain unarmed Aztecs by some of the Spanish soldiers during a religious meeting had resulted in a rebellion. Cortés released Moctezuma in an attempt to quell the angry mobs, who showed their contempt for this action by promptly stoning their emperor to death (it turned out that his subjects had never much liked him anyway!). Hopelessly outnumbered, Cortés was left with no option but to retreat to the territory of nearby allies, although a number of his men were killed as they tried to escape to safety.

Cortés patiently plotted his revenge. Boosting his forces once more through friendly Indians, he marched again for Tenochtitlán in 1521. This time, rather than head straight into the city he besieged it, cutting it off from all outside supplies for many months. The inhabitants succumbed to the Spaniard's military strategy in August and the hostile forces entered the city. They razed it to the ground and in the process prompted the fall of the Aztec empire.

Over the ensuing months and years, Cortés cemented the fate of the Aztec people by stamping Spanish superiority into the provinces and quashing rebellions whenever they arose. Along with their weapons, the Europeans also brought diseases against which the natives had no resistance. Where their swords failed to do the job, smallpox usually finished it. Cortés's gamble on receiving royal pardon for his earlier dissent proved correct after the claiming of one of Latin America's richest prizes in the name of the Spanish king. This in turn ensured further official support for the new territory, making the job of securing it all the more certain.

Interestingly, however, although this support strengthened the Spanish grip on the former Aztec empire, the proliferation of government officials and politicians it brought with it reduced Cortés's own powers and influence to the point where he ultimately returned to Europe frustrated and disillusioned at his treatment. Nevertheless, in the interim he still succeeded in discovering the Tres Marías islands through a Pacific expedition in 1532 and Lower California in 1535–36. In addition, the city he had founded on the former site of Tenochtitlán, Mexico City, grew within only a couple of decades to become one of the most important in Spanish America.

Cortés's legacy was not merely confined to the territory of his own victories either. No doubt inspired by his success over the Aztecs, and by the initial glory heaped on Balboa after his discovery of the Pacific, other conquistadors now came forward to begin subduing the rest of central and southern America. The most notorious of these, and possibly the most cold-blooded, was Balboa's former lieutenant Francisco Pizarro whose own victories went on to match, if not exceed, those of Cortés.

Between 1531 and 1535, after several years of trying to make contact with the empire without much success, Pizarro brought about the conquest and downfall of the great, and fabulously wealthy, Inca civilisation. Ostensibly associated with Peru, the Inca empire at that time actually stretched along the western side of South America from Equador down to Chile. Taking advantage of a civil war between the Incas at the time of his arrival, Pizarro manipulated the empire's rival factions to meet his all-conquering ends. He employed systematic killing, torture and kidnapping to fulfil his goals. Later, he even turned on his Spanish peer, Diego de Almagro, who had been with him during the initial conquest of the Incas, overseeing his execution in order to cement his own position.

However, such devilry could not be sustained forever without some attempt at reprisal. In 1541, Almagro's son and his supporters succeeded in gaining their revenge by assassinating Pizarro, ending his ruthless reign in the most direct manner. But by then disease, dictatorship and the desire for gold had already ensured the destruction of the Inca civilisation which, like Cortés's demolition of the Aztecs, wiped it off the face of the earth forever.

Chapter 5

VINLAND TO THE PACIFIC:

Journey across North America

**The history of North American exploration
typically only begins at the end of the fifteenth
century. What is often overlooked, however, is the
fact that Europeans had already visited the continent
some five hundred years earlier.**

These adventurers had even attempted to begin colonising territory there, but the ultimate failure of the settlements and the lengthy gap before the next visitors arrived meant that their exploits were quickly forgotten. Even now, they are frequently overlooked.

The earliest recorded 'discoverer' of North America, therefore, is not Christopher Columbus or John Cabot, but the Viking Bjarni Herjulfsson. Naturally, Herjulfsson was not even looking for the continent when he found it in around AD 986. Like all good early explorers, he was simply blown off course there by accident while trying to sail to Greenland, itself only landed on for the first time a few years earlier by another Viking, Erik the Red. Herjulfsson was not a particularly curious man by nature. Rather than stop to investigate the new lands he had sighted, he simply turned round and eventually plotted a course back to Greenland. So although he had seen North America, he never actually set foot on it.

That honour was left to Herjulfsson's contemporary and Erik the Red's son, Leif Eriksson. Although Herjulfsson had not been keen to investigate the new lands he had sighted, he had at least recorded his adventure when he eventually arrived in Greenland. A few years later, in around AD 1000, Eriksson decided it was time to find out more about these discoveries and prepared an expedition to follow Herjulfsson's route in reverse. Eriksson made at least three landfalls in North America, based on reports of the places Herjulfsson had seen, at sites he called Helluland ('Land of Flat Stone'), Markland ('Wood Land') and Vinland ('Wineland' or 'Pastureland'). The exact location of each of these is not known for sure and speculation on their whereabouts covers an area of America from as far north as Baffin Island to as far South as Cape Cod in Massachusetts. Of the three, Vinland is the most interesting to historians because this is where Eriksson chose to build a small settlement and overwinter before returning to Greenland in the spring.

Viking remains have subsequently been found in L'Anse au Meadows, Newfoundland. Whether or not this was the site of Eriksson's Vinland remains unclear because other Vikings also made attempts to settle in North America in subsequent years, after hearing Eriksson's positive reports of the land there. These attempts failed, probably due to hostile relations with the native Americans. The new lands were abandoned and accounts of them were largely forgotten until after the Columbus era. Regardless of the exact location of Eriksson's settlement, however, the important fact remains that he was the first European to have for certain led an expedition that landed in North America – half a millennium before his other historical New World 'rivals'.

When they did finally arrive post-Columbus, the story of the exploration of North America would in many respects turn out to be a tale of competition between Britain and France, and, later, the independent United States herself. The Spanish influence was still there too, although this did not penetrate as far as in other parts of the New World and increasingly faded over time.

Nonetheless, Spain was again ahead of the rest of Europe in the initial rush for land in some parts of North America. The conquistadors she sent to the southern and central continents are well documented, but those who ventured north are less remembered. For example, Juan Ponce De Leon, who had also sailed on Columbus's second expedition, discovered and claimed Florida for Spain in 1513. Hernando de Soto, who had been with Pizzaro during the conquest of Peru, followed up on early attempts to colonise Florida with instructions for a thorough exploration and conquest of the territory from 1539 until his death from fever in 1542. In the process of this expedition, de Soto also ventured into South and North Carolina, Georgia, Tennessee and Alabama and 'discovered' and crossed the lower Mississippi river into Arkansas. At exactly the same time, Francisco de Coronado was heading into what are now the states of New Mexico, Arizona, Colorado and Nebraska, unveiling the Grand Canyon in the process. Meanwhile, Juan Rodriguez Cabrillo, who was Portuguese by birth but sailed under Spanish sponsorship, began exploring the Californian coastline in 1542 and eventually reached a northerly limit of Oregon. He was the first European to see and land along much of this region. Although Spain would not always fully exploit this new territory in the way she proceeded to do in South and Central America, it meant that she retained some influence on the development of the northern continent for centuries to come. Indeed, it would be a long time before she would give up, in particular, her claims to territory along the Gulf of Mexico, the present-day Mexican–US border states and the US Pacific coastline.

If the Spanish gradually dropped out of the race for North America and, in the process, their contribution to its exploration became somewhat sidelined, then even more neglected is the early Russian interest in the continent. Russia's eastern extremity almost touches on Alaska at the point of the Bering Strait and so expansion through this route into northern America was a natural progression. Alaska became a Russian colony and one man in particular, Aleksandr Baranov, did a huge amount to increase Russian influence during his effective governorship of the territory between 1788 and 1817. As well as exploring the Alaskan coastline, he journeyed as far south as California where he built Fort Ross and he also ventured to Hawaii.

Indeed, so persistent were the claims of all these competing interests, that it would be well into the nineteenth century before many of them were resolved and Northern American territorial and political boundaries began to resemble their present-day arrangements. It would be even longer before all this land could be said to have been comprehensively explored. Although there were so many countries with so many interests in North America over several centuries, it was the size of the territory and the lie of the land that, above all, held them equally at bay.

John Cabot *(c.1450–c.1498)*

If Columbus opened up the New World for the Spanish, and many conquistadors also made it to the northern continent as well as the central and southern regions, then how is it that much of the population in North America ended up speaking English? The answer, in part at least, lies in the story of John Cabot.

Ironically, Cabot, like Columbus and Vespucci, was an Italian by birth. If Italy had been a united nation in the fifteenth and sixteenth centuries then, given the number of early New World explorers she provided, there is a high probability that the dominant language in both North and South America would now be Italian. In Cabot's day, however, Italy did not exist as a single entity; instead it was a series of small independent city-states which, on their own, did not have the financial or political clout to back major expeditions to claim new lands. So it was that Giovanni Caboto, who was born in Genoa and spent his youth in Venice, ended up seeking sponsorship in England under the anglicised version of his name, John Cabot.

The Italian moved with his family to England in about 1484. This was at around the time that Columbus first devised his 'Enterprise of the Indies', a plan that would have as big an impact on Cabot's own life and fortune as it did on that of its originator. On hearing of the scheme, and on subsequently learning of the success of Columbus's 1492–93 expedition, Cabot too became convinced of the significance of attempting to reach Asia via the west. During his earlier career as a merchant trader throughout the Mediterranean, he had probably encountered Arab counterparts who provided the link to the spices, silks and other riches of the East. In the process they also added their own mark-up and restricted the quantities of those luxury items that made it to Europe. By heading west, Cabot believed, these middlemen could be bypassed altogether and direct trading links with the Indies established.

It is likely that Cabot initially contemplated offering his services, like Columbus, to Spain or Portugal and, if they had been taken up, the subsequent cultural and lingual development of North America might have been very different. As it was, the person who showed the most interest in his scheme was King Henry VII of England: and so began the origins of the British claim on North America.

Perhaps motivated by a need not to be left out of the territorial successes being enjoyed by the Spanish and

Portuguese explorers, perhaps driven merely by the financial incentives of trade with Asia, Henry VII finally bought into Cabot's plan to 'do a Columbus' in 1496. Consequently, he issued Cabot with 'Letters Patent' that gave the explorer

> *full and free authoritie, leave, and power, to sayle to all partes, countreys, and seas, of the East, of the West, and of the North, under our banners ... to seeke out, discover, and finde, whatsoever iles, countreyes, regions or provinces ... in what part of the world soever they be, whiche before this time have beene unknowen to all Christians.*

Nevertheless, the king was keen not to encroach on the Spanish sphere of influence in the southern regions of the New World and so Cabot was to seek out a more northerly route across the Atlantic. This had been within the Italian's design anyway. By crossing the ocean at a higher latitude, he felt certain that he would not only reach Asia but do so more swiftly and easily, because the curve of the earth meant there would be less distance to cover.

Cabot wasted little time in outfitting an expedition to take advantage of his royal grant. With only a single ship, the *Matthew*, and just eighteen crew he left Bristol in May 1497 on what would turn out to be a voyage that was arguably as historic as that of Columbus. When he landed on the North American continent on 24 June 1497, he became the first of the modern wave of New World explorers to actually reach the American mainland. Columbus had by this stage still only made it to the islands off Central America and Vespucci's later claim of a voyage to the South American mainland at around the same time probably never took place. The journey had turned out to be no quicker than Columbus's due to less favourable wind conditions, nor had Cabot found the much sought-after Spice Islands of Asia, but it had brought him to the mainland itself and had in turn given England its significant claim to the territories of North America.

The exact location of Cabot's landing remains unclear and, due to the prestige and potential revenue associated with such a historic event, is something of a controversial topic. Many believe he first landed at Cape Breton in Nova Scotia while others herald the possibilities of Newfoundland, Labrador or a point even as far south as Maine.

Certainly, Cabot went on to explore a significant

section of the eastern American coastline over the following month, before heading home for England. After a brief, unintended detour via Brittany, France he arrived on 6 August 1497. Instead of the hoped-for tales of plentiful spices, his crew brought back stories of fishing waters so abundant that marine life literally jumped into their baskets as soon as they lowered them into the sea. In spite of the disappointment at not finding their intended cargo, Cabot was still hailed as a hero and Henry VII, ever a king with an eye for a bargain, was so pleased with the developments that he was eager to sponsor a follow-up expedition in the following year.

Unfortunately, this journey was far less successful. Although Cabot had a much grander fleet of five ships and up to three hundred men, it did not help his cause. One of the vessels limped back damaged to Ireland early in the voyage, but of the remaining four nothing was ever heard of again. Some think the expedition perhaps made it as far as Greenland and then on to Canada before possibly returning to England. Far more likely, however, is the commonly held belief that at some point during the Atlantic crossing the whole fleet perished and with it John Cabot.

The Cabot name did not die with this doomed second expedition, however. The Italian had three sons, all of whom possibly accompanied him on his first historic voyage to North America. One of these, Sebastian Cabot, went on to establish his own reputation as a navigator and cartographer who also led his own expeditions to the New World. It is possible that he made another voyage to Canada in 1508, although many historians now believe that this journey did not in fact take place.

Sebastian Cabot certainly did, however, lead a fleet to South America between 1526 and 1530. The original objective of the expedition was to repeat Magellan's voyage around the world (*see* page 336) while hoping to find a less trying route around South America, but Cabot became distracted by looking for silver along the Rio de La Plata and Paraná and Paraguay rivers. The consequent perceived failure of his expedition meant that it was some time before his reputation recovered. Nevertheless, once he had given up riding the waves himself he managed to successfully carve out a career as an adviser to other adventurers.

By this time, privateers had long since taken to mimicking John Cabot's route to North America for the dual purpose of trading with the natives and taking advantage of the fish stocks on which he had reported. Worryingly for England, the French had also arrived. What is more, they were also beginning to make their own claims to the territory of North America.

Jacques Cartier *(1491–1557)*

If the English turned up fashionably late to the global exploration party, then the French almost missed it altogether. While the other European powers had long since begun tucking into their New World dinner, France was hardly to be seen. Jacques Cartier was the man who, in 1534, turned up just in time to make sure that his nation made it for at least some of the American pie.

One of the few other French forays of note before this time was, almost inevitably, carried out by an Italian. A decade earlier, Giovanni Da Verrazzano had been commissioned by the French King Francis I to take a look at this New World that was so exciting all the other European powers. He had done well. Verrazzano had journeyed along a significant section of the North American coastline discovering, among other things, New York Bay. He made it as far as Newfoundland in Canada, which was later named 'New France' and claimed on behalf of his sponsor, bringing the French into immediate competition with English American interests.

Although they had been late in arriving, it was an encouraging expedition for the French, but then little else happened for the next ten years. Finally, though, the king decided that it was time for a closer look at 'his' New France. Jacques Cartier, a navigator from St. Malo with a respected reputation, was told to prepare a fleet for an adventure that would see him sail into French-Canadian history.

Like most of the major powers at this time, the king's principal interest actually lay in finding a shorter route through the Americas to the prizes of 'known' Asia. As it turned out, however, these early French expeditions laid the groundwork for an ever-expanding Gallic influence in the New World over the ensuing centuries.

Cartier, therefore, headed to Newfoundland with his two ships and began looking for a way through to the Indies. The efforts by countless adventurers over several centuries to find a route around North America would later become known as the search for the Northwest

Passage. This reached such epic proportions that it has its own dedicated place in the history of exploration (*see* Chapter 6). Cartier, like so many others after him, would initially be disappointed at his lack of progress as he searched in vain around Newfoundland, Belle Isle Strait and the Gulf of St. Lawrence. On a more positive note, however, he made amiable contact with many of the native Indians and succeeded in trading with them.

In spite of the lack of progress in finding a shortcut to Asia, news of Cartier's exploits was warmly received when he returned to his homeland later in 1534. France was gradually becoming as interested in the New World territory itself as in the passage, and Cartier was told to prepare for another expedition the following year.

He had not given up on the idea of a water passage completely, however, and this time focused his attention further up the Gulf of St. Lawrence onto the St. Lawrence River itself. It was a journey that would take Cartier and his 110 men through territory that today encompasses some of the principal cities of French Canada. One of the first stops was the location of what is now Québec but was then the native village of Stadacona. Cartier had encountered some of its Huron inhabitants on his previous voyage, two of whom he had even taken back to France with him in the interim so that they could learn to become interpreters. Again, he was welcomed by its native chief Donnacona. From there Cartier continued upriver to the village of Hochelaga and ascended a nearby mountain, which he named Mont Réal. The present-day city of the same name was later founded in this region.

Realising that this river would also fail to provide him with the passage he still hoped for, however, Cartier retreated to Stadacona and settled in for the winter. It was not a happy time, with scurvy taking hold of, and killing, a number of the crew. Furthermore, when the spring thaw came and Cartier was preparing to return to France, he kidnapped Donnacona and several of his people. They had relayed stories of a rich (and mythical, as it later turned out) kingdom to the north called Saguenay. Cartier took them back to France with him, hoping that their personal accounts would help persuade the king to outfit another expedition in search of Saguenay.

He eventually succeeded but, due to war and other interruptions, was not able to return again to New France until 1541. What is more, this time Cartier was sailing only as part of a large colonisation expedition under the overall command of the Sieur de Roberval. Cartier set sail ahead of his commander and explored much of the same territory that he had seen previously, while he awaited Roberval's arrival so that the attempt to find Saguenay could be made in earnest. As his leader had still not shown up by the spring of 1542, and the once-friendly natives were becoming increasingly hostile towards the French presence, Cartier decided to head for home, only to finally rendezvous with Roberval en route. Roberval wanted him to remain, but Cartier resolved to return to France, leaving the former to search in vain for Saguenay.

Apart from possibly making a brief return to try to find Roberval in the following year, on the orders of the king, an expedition about which little is known, this marked the end of Cartier's exploratory career in Canada. Although the job was far from complete, what he had achieved was to open up a stretch of inland continental North America for the first time, with far-reaching consequences for the future.

It took some years, but the next Frenchman to follow in any kind of official capacity was Samuel de Champlain in the early seventeenth century. In the intervening decades, other French merchants and privateers had begun to unofficially settle 'Cartier's' territory and establish trade with the natives, but it was not until de Champlain that the French built fully on the earlier explorer's discoveries. In 1603, he travelled to Canada for the first time, following in Cartier's footsteps as far as Mont Réal. Between 1604 and 1607 he spent time mapping certain sections of the North American coastline, but it was what happened in the following years that would result in his most important legacies. Appointed Lieutenant Governor, de Champlain founded the cities of Québec in 1608 and Montréal in 1611. In between times he discovered Lake Champlain and went on to explore many other areas of New France including the Ottawa River region. Indeed, Champlain came to be known as the 'Father of New France'. He certainly contributed a huge amount to French dominance in the area and he retained a significant personal influence over the territory until his death in 1635.

By then, one of his charges, a man named Etienne Brulé, had also played his part in expanding France's influence, as the conquest of the interior continued. Brulé was probably the first outsider to view Lake Huron;

he went on to unveil Lake Ontario with Champlain and later on it is possible that he even became the first European to see Lake Superior. He also forged south and reached Chesapeake Bay in what is now the USA, after following the Susquehanna river to its mouth.

Next came French fur traders such as Pierre Esprit Radisson who, driven by the wealth to be had in this newly-developing North American industry, pushed ever further into the interior. He is said to have made it as far west as Minnesota. It is also possible that he found the upper Mississippi River ahead of its more generally recognised discoverer, Louis Joliet.

Another early adventurer was René Robert Cavelier, Sieur de la Salle who arrived in Montréal in 1666. Also in the fur trade, he was a keen explorer, initially concentrating on expansion to the west as well. His greatest achievement, though, came through an expedition that followed the Mississippi to its mouth in 1682, staking a French claim to territory that ran through the heart of the North American continent. He took possession of a stretch of land for France which he named Louisiana after his king, Louis XIV. It would later be colonised by French settlers.

Although each of these developments did not necessarily follow in a coordinated or even continuous fashion, so that it took more than a century and a half to fully establish the French influence across North America, they all had their roots in the pioneering work of Jacques Cartier. His determined investigation of the St. Lawrence River had opened up a route to the North American interior from which all of his successors made their own mark.

The French might have arrived a little late at the New World party, but once there they were determined to stay.

Sir Walter Raleigh (c.1552–1618)

Sir Walter Raleigh would doubtless have had something to say about the arrival of the French in North America. Although his principal loathing was reserved for the Spanish, he was never one to be too discerning when it came to decrying England's European rivals. Indeed, it was Raleigh's determination to make sure England stamped her mark on North America ahead of France or Spain that in large part ensured that his country continued to build on the earlier expeditions of John Cabot. This in turn would cement English claims in the

New World, offer resistance to the French and Spanish influence there and ultimately result in the dominance of the English language across much of North America.

The man who led this crusade had a far more colourful life than that of a simple explorer, however. Indeed, in many cases Sir Walter Raleigh did not even take part in the expeditions with which he is credited. Instead, he was their champion and organiser, offering a momentum to English exploration through his fervent patriotism, his role being much the same as that pioneered for Portugal by Henry the Navigator, more than a century and a half earlier.

Raleigh's early life did not necessarily hint at the epitaph that he would ultimately be accorded within the history of exploration. Born in Devon, England to a reasonably well-to-do family, but one of only limited means, there was little to suggest the dominant role that he would achieve within English court life. This was particularly the case in his earliest years when, as a Protestant during the reign of the staunchly Catholic Queen Mary I, all later meaningful avenues to power would have been denied him on account of his religion had the Queen lived long enough or borne a successor.

As it was, the coming to power of Mary's Protestant half-sister Queen Elizabeth I in 1558 would be a pivotal event in Raleigh's later career. Not only did her similar religious leanings open the door for the adventurer, but it was his favourable personal relationship with the Queen that permitted such a rapid rise in influence.

After an early career in the military, and a brief period studying at Oxford before possibly contemplating a livelihood in law, Raleigh first gained his sea legs in the late 1570s. He was the half-brother of Sir Humphrey Gilbert, who at that time had obtained a patent from Elizabeth I to claim more land for England and begin establishing colonies in North America. Raleigh accompanied him on his early voyages to the region, and it is quite likely that his half-brother's passionate pursuit of the North American cause played an important role in developing Raleigh's own fervour on the subject later on. Gilbert later perished during another colonisation attempt in 1583 and it is almost certainly no coincidence that Raleigh picked up his mantle and became England's New World lobbyist from this date.

By this time, Raleigh had firmly established himself in the royal court. After his period at sea with Gilbert, Raleigh had led successful campaigns in Ireland which, coupled with a skill for making political allies and obtaining the requisite introductions, had gradually brought him to the attention of the Queen. The substantial financial and territorial rewards he received from Elizabeth for his service in Ireland give an indication of his growing popularity with her. In 1583 and 1584, by which stage Raleigh was firmly situated among the Queen's favourites, property in London, a monopoly grant on the export of woollen cloth and a knighthood were among his other royal awards. Now Raleigh had both the Queen's ear and purse, it was also at this time that he was permitted to send out his first expedition to the New World in an attempt to succeed where Gilbert had struggled.

Armed with his own patent to explore the New World territories in March 1584, within a month, Raleigh had sent Arthur Barlowe and Philip Amadas out on an investigative expedition to the region. They landed first in Florida, then tracked the coastline as far as North Carolina.

The relative success of this exploration meant that Raleigh wasted no time in organising a follow-up colonization attempt in some of the territory Barlowe and Amadas had examined. In 1585, Sir Richard Grenville was ordered by Raleigh to take a group of settlers to Roanoke Island, North Carolina and establish a permanent English presence there. Although the expedition reached its destination, and also undertook some additional exploration of the American coastline further north, the colony struggled and the majority of the inhabitants chose to return when Sir Francis Drake (*see* page 345) visited the settlement a year later, on his way back from a separate New World expedition.

In 1587, Raleigh tried again in the same area with a new party of settlers, under the governorship of a man called John White who had also been with the first colonization attempt. It resulted in one of the greatest, still unresolved intrigues in early North American history. After arriving and establishing a base, the settlers were left to their own devices by White until, in 1590, he returned to Roanoke Island on a ship with supplies. All he found, however, was a deserted settlement with no sign of the colonists. No-one still knows for sure what happened to them.

Raleigh's attention, however, now turned to South America and an opportunity of the sort he always relished; one where he could both undermine the Spanish and increase his wealth at the same time. On this occasion he personally sailed across the Atlantic, reaching South America in 1595. His goal was the Orinoco river in Venezuela in search of 'El Dorado' and the vast deposits of gold its legend promised. Amongst the more notable legacies of the expedition was his published narrative of the journey, *The Discovery of Guiana*, but sadly not the gold he was seeking. After a gap of more than twenty years, he tried again in 1617, promising his cash-strapped monarch that he would return from the Orinoco with the discovery of a gold mine which, at the same time, would not intrude on Spanish territorial claims. It was a promise that would cost him his head, for in the intervening two decades Raleigh had spent most of his time imprisoned in the Tower of London hoping for a reprieve from a conviction for treason that carried the death sentence. In 1603 Elizabeth I had died and, on the accession of James I to the throne, Raleigh immediately fell from grace within the royal court. Far worse, Raleigh was implicated later the same year in an attempt to overthrow the new king and it is this that led to his detention.

After years of attempting to devise a plan that would allow him to charm his way into release, however, Raleigh finally succeeded with the Orinoco promise. James I needed the money and was prepared to give Raleigh his freedom so that he could attempt to bring the gold home. If, however, he came into conflict with the Spanish in the process who, much to Raleigh's chagrin, the monarch was keen not to antagonise, King James assured him that he would finally enforce his earlier execution order.

The promise was a bold one that even Raleigh himself knew he could probably not keep. Even if he had succeeded in finding gold, he would have found it almost impossible not to impinge on the by now well-established Spanish colonial interests in the area and the Spanish even pointed out as much before his departure. Yet it bought Raleigh the freedom for one last adventure and he was determined to go, come what may.

It was the disaster it promised to be. Raleigh fell ill on the outward journey and was subsequently not even involved in the consequent quest up the Orinoco river itself, remaining instead at nearby Trinidad to recover. The expedition pressed on, however, straight into the domain of the Spanish, began fighting with them and lost Sir Walter's own son in the struggle, among others. No mine was found and on returning to Raleigh with news of the failure, the loss and the conflict, the captain who had led the fleet in his absence, Lawrence Keymis, killed himself. Eventually, Raleigh returned to England in 1618. Inevitably, both the Spanish and James I himself levelled against Raleigh the piracy accusations he had sworn to avoid and the king followed through on his own promise to put the explorer to death for his fleet's conduct. 'This is a sharp Medicine', Raleigh is said to have stated just before his execution, as he viewed the fatal axe that would shortly sever his head from his body, 'but it is a Physician for all Diseases.'

Raleigh's demise represented a sorry end for the man who, driven by both a patriotism and xenophobia rarely rivalled among his contemporaries, had tried so hard to establish his country's territorial rights in the New World. Although he had often been less than successful in the practical application of his expeditions, his undertaking of them in themselves, his attempts at colonisation in North America and his passionate promotion of England's need to be among the powers in the New World would prove to be important actions in his nation's long-term establishment of interests there.

And, by mere coincidence and good fortune, Raleigh

himself would no doubt have conceded with a wry smile, they were actions that just so happened to greatly antagonise England's French and Spanish New World rivals.

Meriwether Lewis *(1774–1809)* and William Clark *(1770–1838)*

By the turn of the nineteenth century, the recently formed independent United States was beginning to flourish. At this point, though, her reach was limited to the eastern third of her present-day territory, so it is little wonder that an overland exploratory mission from the Atlantic end of what is now the USA to the Pacific had yet to take place. Within a few years, though, the 'Lewis and Clark expedition' had achieved just that in perhaps the single most famous exploratory undertaking in North America's history.

Meriwether Lewis, William Clark and the small band of men who comprised the US 'Corps of Discovery' were not, however, the first to complete an overland crossing of the North American continent. That honour belonged to a Scot, Alexander MacKenzie, who had become the first known explorer to traverse the continental divide in Canadian territory in 1793. He had been sent out by his employer, the North West Company, to look for a possible route across North America for trading purposes. A viable commercial passage across the continent linking the markets of Asia, America and Europe together would be invaluable. In addition, it would enhance the claims of Britain, the enterprise's 'home' country, to territory in the Pacific Northwest: territory upon which many leading figures in the United States also had their long-term eye. Although MacKenzie was successful in crossing the continent, he realised that his route was not, however, a viable commercial passage.

Nevertheless, MacKenzie's feat and the subsequent publication of his journal in 1801 spurred the United States, specifically President Thomas Jefferson, into action. If the British could cross the continent, then the US was duty bound to do the same. This would not only snatch away a prized commercial route from European hands but also help cement territorial claims that could lead towards Jefferson's vision of a USA that one day would stretch from coast to coast. So began plans for what would become the Lewis and Clark expedition.

By 1803, a second significant event had occurred

that would give added justification to the proposed undertaking. In that year, the US completed the purchase of 'Louisiana' from Napoleon's France (which had only just prised it from Spanish hands), a portion of North American territory that in those days was loosely defined as stretching from the Mississippi River to the Rocky Mountain Range. Much of Louisiana was unexplored in any detail and Jefferson wanted to know what he had obtained for his multi-million dollar outlay. It also gave the US more authority than ever to explore the central and western side of the continent and in the process spread the word throughout Louisiana of the US's new sovereignty in the region.

By this stage, Jefferson had already selected Captain Meriwether Lewis to head up a US expedition of investigation and exploration across the continent. Lewis was a young Virginia planter who had joined the army and had later spent time serving as President Jefferson's private secretary. As part of his preparations for the mission, Lewis was instructed to begin putting together a small team – probably only a dozen or so men – including a Lieutenant as second-in-command.

At this stage, however, Lewis did a remarkable thing.

He voluntarily gave up sole overall authority of the expedition to offer a joint command on equal terms to his former military colleague William Clark. It would turn out to be one of the most successful partnerships in exploration history. In fact, due to administrative and political complications, it later transpired that Clark officially remained a Lieutenant and second-in-command in the eyes of the government, but to all those in the Corps of Discovery, most of all to Meriwether Lewis himself, he was 'Captain' Clark and co-leader of the great undertaking.

As the man initially appointed to head the mission, however, Lewis undertook most of the early preparations during 1803. Towards the end of the year he journeyed along the Ohio River from Pittsburgh with much of the equipment he had prepared, meeting up with Captain Clark near the Ohio falls. Before the end of the year, the party had ascended the Mississippi just beyond St. Louis, where they set up camp for the winter. Although the mission had officially already started, it would not begin in earnest until the following spring when it moved away from St. Louis, its last contact with a significant, established town.

The mission for the Corps of Discovery, by now numbering thirty-plus porters and other companions for the first leg of the journey, was to follow the Missouri River across the continent to its source. From there they would seek as short a passage across the Rocky Mountains as possible, aiming to quickly pick up the Columbia River, some of which had been charted by previous explorers along the Pacific coast, and descend it to the Ocean. Apart from being an ideally short overland traversing of the Rockies, the hope was that the route would turn out to be a practical all-water crossing of the American continent which would open up commerce from coast to coast. This would leave the United States in a beneficial trading position from which it could force out its competitors in the region.

It was a mammoth task by any standards, even more so in 1804. In an age before steam power was available to Lewis and Clark, the Corps of Discovery had to row or drag their equipment and boats thousands of miles upstream for the majority of the outward journey. Typically, they had to hunt daily to ensure that enough provisions were available to feed themselves. Increasingly, as they travelled further from St. Louis, they were struggling through uncharted territory, under constant fear of native Indian attack. Indeed, beyond the primary exploratory and commercial goals of the expedition, Lewis and Clark had been specifically instructed to observe and make contact with the rival Indian nations, to encourage them to make peace with each other, to inform them of US sovereignty and, ideally, to establish friendly relations between east and west. Understandably, it was not always a message that went down well with the natives, many of whom had already established some kind of trading relations with the British, the French or the Spanish which they did not want to forfeit; they also feared US invasion of their territories.

Nevertheless, certain Indian tribes were more cordial than others to the band of explorers. In particular, Lewis and Clark established good relations with the Mandans who resided in what is now North Dakota. This was the location along the Missouri that the Corps had reached towards the end of 1804, so they took the opportunity to set up winter camp there, constructing a dwelling they named Fort Mandan. They had enjoyed mixed fortunes with other natives at earlier points along the river, notably struggling in their dealings with certain Sioux Indians, but at least they had avoided all-out hostilities and they continued to make progress. Indeed, so far they had only lost one man – the only one they would lose on the entire expedition – and that was to illness not attack.

After a hard but successful winter at Fort Mandan the party was divided into two, as had always been planned by the Captains. A number of men and porters were sent back to St. Louis to carry news of the expedition's progress so far, as well as an invaluable map of the territory they had charted, together with other reports. Indeed, on top of all the other responsibilities of the expedition, Lewis and Clark had also been instructed to complete a number of scientific tasks, so they took the opportunity to dispatch details of their findings on this front too. One of their most important scientific targets was to seek out and describe previously undiscovered flora and fauna. Lewis in particular excelled in this area and dispatched a large quantity of samples, specimens and accounts with the returning group.

The remaining members – some thirty-one in number, including translators, Clark's black slave York and a native Indian woman and guide called Sacagawea – formed the 'permanent party' which would go on to the Pacific Ocean. As they went off in the opposite direction to their homebound colleagues, in April 1805, they were aware that they probably had the toughest part of their expedition ahead of them. They probably did not realise, however, quite how tough it would be.

As well as the ongoing, gruelling drive upstream towards the source of the Missouri, they would undertake a time-consuming and arduous land portage around the river's Great Falls. Moreover, they next had to cross the Rocky Mountains, a task that the majority of the Indians they encountered in the region told them would be impossible. Nevertheless, they managed to find one old native who claimed to have made the crossing and who was willing to act as their guide for much of the journey. They succeeded in making the treacherous crossing with his help, but not without encountering severe hardship and lack of food in the process.

The party eventually found its way via the Clearwater and Snake Rivers to the Columbia which, if nothing else, at least had the advantage of flowing in the direction in which they were travelling. In November 1805, they at last reached the target of their travails, the mouth of the Columbia. They had crossed what is now the United States and had arrived at the Pacific Ocean.

Although they had succeeded in their goal with great leadership, teamwork, native assistance and not a little luck, the expedition's work was only halfway complete. Now they had to return home safely again. Initially there had been thoughts of possibly hailing a passing ship that would take them round Cape Horn and back to the east coast, but there were none in the vicinity. Besides, Lewis and Clark wanted to undertake additional exploration on the way home. This, however, involved splitting the party into several smaller teams for a period, with all the added risk of attack that such a decision implied.

Having camped through the winter at Fort Clatsop on the Pacific Coast, the Corps headed eastwards again in March 1806. Unfortunately, a particularly heavy winter and consequent delay in the melting of the snow meant that they were held up near the foot of the Bitterroot section of the Rocky Mountains for several weeks before they could attempt a crossing. Luckily, they were waiting in the territory of the Nez Percé Indians with whom they had established excellent relations such that, after they had initially struggled on their own, they were able to persuade a number of the locals to eventually guide them back across the Bitterroots.

It was at this point that the Corps fanned out into its separate sub-groupings in order to further investigate the most direct route across the remainder of the Rocky range as well as the course of certain rivers that deposited into the Missouri. When they met up again, just over a month later, all had encountered difficulties and incidents but none had been quite so dramatic as the experience of Lewis's breakaway team of just four men. As this party investigated the Marias River in the hope that it would extend into Canadian territory and thereby give the United States a claim to push the territorial boundary further north, they encountered eight Blackfoot Indians. Initially relations were civil, but after the two groups had camped together the Indians attempted to steal the guns of Lewis's men at first light on the following morning. A scuffle broke out, shots were fired and in the process one Indian was stabbed to death and another was seriously wounded. The Indians retreated, probably to seek more help, at which point Lewis's hopelessly outnumbered party raced day and night on horseback, almost without stop, to be sure of escaping without reprisals.

Fortunately when all the sub-groupings met up again in August on the Missouri River before heading for home, further occurrences of this explicitly hostile nature were avoided en route. With the current in their favour now, they raced for St. Louis before the winter set in again. Although speedy progress was made the journey was, nonetheless, not entirely without incident, not least when Lewis was shot through the backside. He had been shot, probably in error, by one of his own men on a hunting foray, just as the teams were reuniting! The great co-leader of the expedition spent most of the remainder of the journey home lying in a boat on his front, waiting for the big bullet holes in his behind to heal.

Towards the end of September 1806, however, the Corps of Discovery returned triumphant to St. Louis. Many had given them up for dead, making the homecoming celebrations all the more exultant. They had completed one of the great exploratory missions of all time and had firmly helped establish the basis of the future expansion of the United States across the continent. Other celebrated names in the history of the American West such as Zebulon Pike, Jim Bridger and Jedediah Strong Smith would soon go on to build on their achievements and uncover more of the unknown lands. Lewis, Clark and the entire Corps of Discovery were gratefully rewarded with extra pay and land grants by the government for their bravery, contribution to knowledge and exemplary service on behalf of their nation. Lewis was made Governor of Louisiana and Clark Superintendent of Indian Affairs in the same territory.

Unfortunately, lows would almost inevitably follow such highs, at least in the case of Lewis. While Clark went on to become highly regarded in his new role, found himself a wife and soon had children, Lewis struggled with his responsibilities. He took to drinking more and more, he took too many drugs for his ailments and to help him sleep and he let his financial affairs spiral out of control. In addition, he failed to write up and publish the long-awaited journals after he had promised Jefferson and Clark that he would personally produce them on behalf of both the captains. Lewis afterwards fell into a depression and is believed to have shot himself (although some believe he was murdered) and he died in October 1809.

America had lost one of its all-time heroes at just thirty-five years of age, and with him much of the first-hand knowledge of the new territories to the west. Yet, in large part, because of Lewis and Clark's groundbreaking adventures with the Corps of Discovery, the march westwards had become more of a driving force than ever.

It would not stop until the rest of the nation of the United States had caught up and North America's lines of demarcation took the form in which they are recognized today.

Chapter 6
A TRADE ROUTE TO THE EAST:
In search of the Northwest Passage

The Northwest Passage is the term that became associated with the repeated attempts by explorers to find a sea route around the North American continent to the trade riches of 'known' Asia.

In a way, the quest for the Northwest Passage began as soon as Columbus set out westwards in search of his more direct route to the Indies in 1492. This was even more the case when John Cabot deliberately charted a northerly course across the Atlantic in the hope of finding Asia in 1497. Yet although these men were searching for what the Northwest Passage came to represent – a shortcut to the East – they were simply looking for a route, any route, at whatever latitude, to the Orient. At this stage the Northwest Passage had not been specifically identified as the only hope of finding a natural waterway through the New World to the Indies, short of the long detour around South America.

In 1534 the Frenchman Jacques Cartier was one of the first men who arguably set out with the specific goal of finding some kind of Northwest Passage around a North American continent that was already known to be there. Yet he, and those of his fellow countrymen who later followed him, quickly became distracted by the more intriguing, and ultimately more fruitful, prospect of exploring and settling 'New France'. With this diversion then, the French interest in finding the Passage gradually waned.

So it was left to the British to pick up the baton again, renewing their interest in the New World and, more specifically, a northern route to the East, during the Elizabethan era. They would spearhead yet more attempts in the seventeenth century, with even the odd foray in the eighteenth century, when perceived wisdom by then suggested that even if such a Northwest Passage did exist, it would be frozen over for much of the time and consequently of limited commercial use. Perceived wisdom counted for nothing, however, for the newly optimistic, and soon to be equally disappointed, wave of British explorers of the nineteenth century who turned the enduring quest for the Passage into an epic tale. Their exploits are principally the reason that this channel came to have a unique place, and chapter, of its own in the conquest of the unknown; although logically this straightforward search for a route around America should only have merited a footnote in the history of exploration.

In the end, for all the centuries of British effort, it was left to a Norwegian, Roald Amundsen (*see* page 291) to complete the first navigation of the Northwest Passage in its entirety in 1905. Ironically, Amundsen was such a competent and comprehensive explorer of polar regions that the accomplishment that so many before him had yearned for and died for is usually listed as a mere minor achievement in any summary of his career.

Yet that, in a way, is perhaps only fitting after all. The Northwest Passage is indeed just a channel through only one small portion of the world's surface, all of which had to be discovered and explored at some point. But it is there and it was difficult. And that is why so many great explorers threw their lives at it.

Sir Martin Frobisher *(c.1535–1594)*

Sir Martin Frobisher was not the first, and would certainly not be the last, to attempt the navigation of a Northwest Passage around the American continent to Asia. He did, however, represent the re-engagement of England in the quest to find this elusive thoroughfare and he subsequently sparked a revival of his nation's interest both in North America itself and in finding a shortcut around it.

Born in Altofts in Yorkshire, England, Frobisher attained his station by working his way up through the ranks. He began his maritime career as a cabin boy in

1544, spending much of his youth aboard vessels on expeditions to Africa and becoming involved in attacks on French trading ships. Indeed, so devoutly did he pursue this latter course that he was accused of piracy on a number of occasions during the 1560s, although he always managed to avoid being tried for his conduct. By 1565, he had ascended to the rank of captain. His interest by now had already started to turn westwards across the Atlantic, but it would be more than a decade before he could put together the fleet that would take him there.

Frobisher was not the only one who was contemplating a revival of English interest in the Northwest Passage during the 1560s. Sir Humphrey Gilbert, Walter Raleigh's half brother, wrote a short text in 1566 entitled *A Discourse of a Discovery for a New Passage to Cataia*. With this pamphlet, he hoped to persuade Queen Elizabeth I to have England re-enter the hunt for a Northwest (or even Northeast) Passage to Asia. The queen was not for rushing, however, and although Gilbert would eventually be granted his chance, it did not materialise until 1578. On the other hand, the treatise added momentum and inspiration to Frobisher's own plans to undertake a similar task. Progress, however, was barely any quicker for him. Through the patronage of the Earl of Warwick, and even some of Gilbert's own funds, he eventually received his opportunity in 1576.

So it was he set sail with three vessels from London to the New World on 7 June 1576. It was a tough outward journey. The smallest of the ships was lost in the early stages of the crossing. Then, on seeing the size of some of the icebergs and other horrors of the north that they would encounter, the crew of the *Michael*, one of the two larger remaining boats, deserted. Frobisher would not be thwarted, however, and he pressed on for the Passage with his solitary vessel, the *Gabriel*.

Towards the end of July he reached what is now known as Frobisher Bay, an inlet about 150 miles long on Baffin Island, Canada, which leads to nothing more than a dead end. Convinced he had at last found the Passage through to Asia, however, he named it 'Frobisher's Strait' and began sailing down it although, unfortunately, not to its futile conclusion.

Indeed, the attempt at the Passage would end sooner than Frobisher would have liked, following a difficult encounter with native Inuit Indians as he explored the bay. At first, as they rowed towards his ship in their kayaks, they appeared to be welcoming the strangers. Later, though, they kidnapped five members of Frobisher's crew who, in spite of later rescue attempts, were never seen again.

Deciding to quit while he was still marginally ahead, Frobisher turned for home to report his findings before winter fully set in. In addition to the prized Passage he believed he had identified, a late bonus had also been encountered in the form of the discovery of lumps of a black mineral which was believed to contain gold ore. It was potentially a double win: treasures to be had in the New World itself and treasures to be had from known Asia through 'Frobisher's Strait'.

Again, like so many before and after him, Frobisher would ultimately be disappointed. Initially, on his arrival back in England in October, though, his news was received with great excitement. Such was the enthusiasm, admittedly more for the prospect of easy gold pickings than immediately completing the navigation of the Passage, that even the queen was moved to contribute to the outfitting of a new and more substantial expedition in the following year.

Departing in late May 1577 and again arriving at Frobisher Bay in July, the principal aim of this second voyage was commercial. Although it also formally claimed for England the territories Frobisher had encountered, land which the queen herself later named 'Meta Incognita', little progress was made on the Passage. Instead, the party was content to stop again at Frobisher Bay, mine 200 tons of the black mineral they had previously encountered and return fully laden to England in September: overloaded with riches, they hoped.

Still the bubble had not burst. Frobisher was sent out again in the following year, this time with fifteen vessels and enough men and miners to begin a colony in the new territory. If there was time, perhaps they would investigate the Northwest Passage just a little further, although this had again been placed lower down the list of immediate priorities. As it turned out, Frobisher navigated more of the waters around northern Canada than he had initially intended because on his arrival in the region he erroneously sailed for sixty miles along the channel of water to the south of Baffin Island now known as the Hudson Strait. Reluctantly, for Frobisher himself was still partly motivated by a desire to complete a passage through to Asia, he eventually turned his back on this promising channel, naming it 'Mistaken Strait', before faithfully returning to his duties on the shores of Frobisher Bay. More ore was had and more fully laden vessels departed for England in the autumn.

It would be a disappointing homecoming. Back in England, the news had at last broken that the minerals that had so distracted Frobisher's second and third expeditions from completing the Passage did not in fact contain gold, but were merely iron pyrites, or 'fool's gold'. The hoards were worthless. The game was up for Frobisher and his Northwest Passage adventures. He never again returned to the region. Instead he spent most of the rest of his career antagonizing French and Spanish shipping throughout the Atlantic and elsewhere, as all prominent English Elizabethan mariners were almost duty bound to do. His service against the Spanish during the attempted Armada invasion of 1588 also earned him a knighthood. It would ultimately, however, earn him an early grave in 1594 when he was badly injured near the Azores in a raid on a Spanish ship carrying gold. He died from his wounds shortly afterwards.

In spite of the anti-climactic outcome of Frobisher's North American forays, the fool's gold revelation did not stop the English. On the contrary, a new wave of interest in the region had been sparked. Gilbert picked up the baton from Frobisher, and Raleigh in turn picked it up from his half-brother. While they concentrated more on the North American continent itself, though, others were keen to pick up on the potential channels to Asia that Frobisher had unveiled. John Davis was the next to try in the 1580s, discovering the Davis Strait between Baffin Island and Greenland during his endeavours. In the early seventeenth century, Henry Hudson examined the promising strait through to the enormous Hudson Bay that Frobisher had unveiled and which now bears his name. Thomas Button, William Gibbons, Robert Bylot and William Baffin all tried too. After realizing that the Hudson Strait route would not provide the Passage, the last two instead continued through the Davis Strait into Baffin Bay and northwards up Smith Sound before being thwarted by ice. Not long afterwards, Luke Foxe would have his turn at the Passage but would again be disappointed at the dead end that is now known as the Foxe Basin.

The hunt was on in earnest for the Northwest Passage. It would go on. And on.

Sir William Edward Parry *(1790–1855)*

William Edward Parry was a remarkable man. In an age before steam, electric lighting and specialist snow equipment, he penetrated the ice of the Northwest Passage further than anyone else, spent several winters in the sunless Arctic and made an attempt on the North Pole which would not be bettered for fifty years. And yet, he would doubtless be the first to say, he was just doing his duty.

Parry was one of the first of a new wave of British explorers who, among other tasks, were sent out to finally conquer the Northwest Passage in the first half of the nineteenth century. In spite of repeated attempts to find the still much-prized channel over several hundred years, above all else by Britain, it had remained stubbornly out of reach. In fact, although seemingly endless time, money and lives had already been expended on the quest, explorers had still barely penetrated the Passage to any degree. There was, of course, a reason for this. A Northwest Passage does exist through the maze of islands and straits around North America, but it is perpetually frozen, and hence useless to any practical extent. Later representatives of the earlier wave of explorers, such as William Baffin, had already come to this conclusion and, for a time, interest in conquering the Passage again waned. By the nineteenth century, however, the analyses of Baffin and his contemporaries were being called into question and the British navy decided that it was time to start all over again. William Parry, in essence, was selected to be the man at the forefront of this new wave of optimism.

On his first expedition to the Northwest Passage, however, Parry was only second-in-command. The year was 1818 and, in his late twenties, he was still young. Much better, the navy concluded, to head it with a man of greater maritime experience and years. So they chose Sir John Ross, uncle of Sir James Clark Ross (*see* page 209). In time, John Ross would also be seen as being among the greatest, and certainly among the most persistent, of those explorers who threw themselves at the Northwest Passage in the first half of the nineteenth century. But it would take him a long time to re-establish his reputation after his initial unsuccessful attempt in 1818, for which

ABOVE: *An illustrated map depicting the journey of the Venetian merchant Marco Polo along the Silk Road to China.*

BELOW: *Vasco da Gama introduces himself to the court of Calicut, India, 1498. Although da Gama was initially well received, relations between explorer and hosts did not remain good.*

ABOVE: *The Cape of Good Hope, the southernmost tip of the African continent. A combination of currents from north and south around this cape makes navigation treacherous in the extreme.*

BELOW: *The road to Timbuktu, a fifty-two day camel ride away, according to this desert signpost.*

ABOVE: *Columbus is greeted by South American natives on his arrival in the New World. He would quickly outstay his welcome amongst his hosts, however.*

ABOVE: Seizing the Inca of Peru, *painting by John Everett Millais showing Pizarro's capture of the Inca ruler Atahuallpa.*

BELOW: *John and Sebastian Cabot land on the North American continent, 1497. The exact spot of Cabot's landfall is unknown.*

ABOVE: *Lewis and Clark with their teenage Shoshone Indian guide, Sacagawea. Although she has received little recognition, without Sacagawea's help, it is unlikely the expedition would have got far.*

RIGHT: *Fridtjof Nansen meets English explorer Frederick Jackson on Franz Josef Land, a chance meeting which almost certainly saved the lives of Nansen and his companion Hjalmar Johanssen.*

LEFT: *Ernest Shackleton's* Endurance *trapped in the Antarctic ice, 1915. Although the* Endurance *was built for exactly this kind of situation, eventually the ice won the battle.*

BELOW: *Scott's expedition party: (l to r) Laurence Oates, H.R. Bowers, Robert Scott, Edward Wilson and Edgar Evans. Successful in their attempt to reach the South Pole, the party would find the return journey too far.*

LEFT: *Captain James Cook, the Yorkshire-born explorer, navigator and cartographer who ended the debate as to the existence of the Australian continent by landing on it.*

BELOW: *Edmund Hillary and Tenzing Norgay enjoy a snack prior to their ascent of Everest, 1953.*

the Admiralty, press and British public slated him alike.

The British did not mind failure. In fact, where the Northwest Passage was concerned, they almost certainly expected it. But any unsuccessful attempt had to be a glorious failure. The more hardship that had been endured in not quite making it, the better. Sir John Franklin (*see* page 200) would build his reputation on such a basis. William Parry fully understood the concept too. James Clark Ross, in certain aspects of his exploratory career, was almost in danger of succeeding, but he also made sure that he endured enough desolate winters in the Arctic to be forgiven those minor indiscretions.

In 1818, however, John Ross proved that he had not yet quite grasped the concept. With instructions to sail into Baffin Bay and on through either Smith Sound, Jones Sound or the most promising passage, Lancaster Sound, he did just that. But on arriving at these potential channels, he decided incorrectly and without full investigation that each was a bay. So having followed his orders, and with nowhere else to go, he turned around and, only seven months after departing, was back in England having suffered no hardship whatsoever. It would take fifteen years in the societal wilderness before the British public would forgive him. Only then was Ross redeemed because he so successfully managed to trap himself in the ice off North America that it took him four years (1829–33) and the loss of his ship before he escaped just in the nick of time to avoid starvation and scurvy. On this occasion, of course, he returned a hero.

Although present on the failed 1818 expedition, William Parry, by contrast, was deemed to have accomplished himself with proper, and appropriately subordinate, conduct, such that he could not in any way be blamed for the party's inglorious failure. Consequently, when a return expedition was approved to leave the following year, Ross was dropped and Parry installed at its command. It would be the most successful of all his attempts at the Northwest Passage and, indeed, the most accomplished effort by anyone to date.

He left with two ships in May 1819, the *Hecla* and the *Griper*, and by the beginning of August he had made his way through the dense ice in the centre of Baffin Bay to the entrance of Lancaster Sound. Unlike Ross, Parry was prepared, indeed ordered, to sail and keep on sailing through it until he encountered either land or ice head-on. As it turned out, he was stopped on this stretch by neither. Lancaster Sound was not a bay at all, but a channel. By proving this alone, Parry had already secured iconic status for himself and at the same time ensured that John Ross's ruin, for the next decade at least, would be complete.

Eventually, a good couple of hundred miles further west than Ross had managed, Parry's way was temporarily blocked by ice at a place he had called Barrow Strait, after one of his chief Admiralty mentors and patrons, Sir John Barrow. He took the opportunity to return to explore some of the other inlets he had discovered on his way west, most notably one that he had called Prince Regent Inlet. It seemed to offer an alternative passage in the future should Barrow Strait remain perpetually blocked. Indeed, it was in the deepest depths of Prince Regent Inlet that Sir John Ross would spend most of his time trapped in ice during his redemption period of 1829–33.

As it was, Barrow Strait opened up again and Parry continued his ground-breaking journey westwards from late August. Before winter set in they managed another couple of hundred miles in that direction. In the process they crossed the significant meridian of 110 degrees west, collecting the prize of £5,000 that had been put up by the British Parliament for any expedition reaching that milestone in pursuit of the Northwest Passage. There would be a further £20,000 awaiting them if they made it all the way to the Pacific.

In the interim, though, the team would have to endure an Arctic winter iced in at a newly-discovered landfall that Parry had named Melville Island. He had planned for such an event, indeed he had expected that it would take at least two 'navigable' seasons to make his way through channels that for much of the year were blocked by ice. So he established winter quarters as best he could: he would have to await the spring thaw in the darkness of the almost constant Arctic night before he was able to continue on his way.

Between Melville Island and what is now known to be Banks Island, there is indeed a land free channel that extends all the way to 'open' sea and further along the North American coastline to the Bering Strait and the Pacific Ocean. Unfortunately this route is continually blocked by ice. So when the thaw finally came at the end of July 1820, which permitted Parry to briefly carry on along his way, he very quickly found that his intended path westward was again thwarted by impenetrable barriers of icebergs. Indeed, he had been lucky in ever having been able to journey as far as Melville Island in the unusually mild conditions of the previous year and was now at risk of being trapped indefinitely in the Arctic ice. Acknowledging that it was time to concede defeat, and doubtless, at least subconsciously, realising that he had endured hardship enough during the previous winter to be hailed for his heroic failure on his return to Britain, he turned for home. Zipping eastwards as fast as he could go in order to avoid the encroaching ice, he escaped the Arctic in the nick of time and was back in Britain by the end of October.

Parry had failed to complete the Northwest Passage, but he had gloriously failed and that was arguably even better. In a single expedition, he had conquered more of the Passage than any other explorer, he had proved that Lancaster Sound was navigable and he had competently endured a winter further north than any known European before him. The fact that he had been pipped at the post by the ice off Melville Island made for an even better hard luck story and it still left the way open for more exciting and equally doomed attempts at the Passage.

Indeed, Parry himself was to lead the next two expeditions. Sadly, they were far less gloriously unsuccessful than his first stab but because he had done so well during his initial expedition he at least survived with some of his reputation intact. The second endeavour with Parry in command resulted in two winters, from 1821 to 1823, being spent in the Arctic ice. Realising that the route through Barrow Strait and Melville Island would always ultimately be thwarted by ice, he decided to retrace the steps of the early explorers further south, through Hudson Strait and Foxe Basin, in the hope of finding a passage that they had missed. He almost got lucky. Parry's team found a previously undiscovered channel that ran westwards out of Foxe Basin which he named the Fury and Hecla Strait, after his two ships. But thick banks of ice again made the narrow passage all but unnavigable so, after more than two years of trying, Parry was forced to return home having not even managed to come close to his previous furthest west record.

His third expedition was even less successful. Between 1824 and 1825, Parry decided to make a thorough attempt on the Prince Regent Inlet that he had previously discovered. Just making his way into the inlet during the summer of 1824 involved him in many difficulties and he barely managed to explore fifty miles of it before the ice became so thick that he had to bed in for the winter. Eventually, by July 1825, the ships were freed by the Arctic summer again. Only a further fifty or so miles were completed, however, before a combination of icebergs and storms wrecked the *Fury*, one of Parry's two ships. With two crews on a single ship, and only half the supplies that were required, Parry had to concede defeat and head back to Britain. Again, little knowledge had been added beyond that already gained during his first expedition. Parry never attempted the Northwest Passage again.

He was not completely finished with the Arctic, however. His Admiralty masters had one last job for their dutiful explorer. In 1827, they despatched him for an attempt on the North Pole. Without ever coming close to completing its stated goal the expedition still achieved just enough, in difficult circumstances, to restore any damage done to Parry's reputation by his last two Northwest Passage attempts. In fact, given the age in which he was undertaking the challenge and the unsophisticated equipment he had at his disposal, he did remarkably well. Ultimate testimony to this would be that nobody managed to beat Parry's furthest north record for another fifty years. But he did not, of course, make the Pole. He made 82 degrees 45 minutes latitude, still five hundred miles short of the top of the world, before a combination of exhaustion, dwindling food supplies and a southward-heading ice flow, which meant they were almost moving backwards, persuaded Parry to stop. For over a month, his team had man-hauled – the reindeer they had brought with them not being up to the job – two unwieldy 'amphibious' boats and their supplies all that distance from their starting point on the northerly island of Spitsbergen. It was time to go home. And, on this occasion, it was time for Parry to hang up his Arctic boots altogether.

Sir John Franklin *(1786–1847)*

Sir John Franklin knew a thing or two about attempts on the North Pole. Indeed, his Arctic calling had begun with such an expedition. In a reverse pattern to Parry, he graduated from this adventure to multiple attempts on the Northwest Passage. It was a challenge that would both boost and literally end his career in an even more dramatic fashion than Parry's own exploits had.

The North Pole attempt had taken place in 1818, with Franklin second-in-command to a man named David Buchan. Unlike Parry's later stab at the same goal, this initial effort would be far less successful. Indeed, Franklin achieved less than Parry in every endeavour he undertook and yet he arguably ended his career more lauded and more praised than his compatriot. This was perhaps because Franklin, of all the new wave of Northwest Passage explorers, was the man who all but wrote the guidebook on the heroic failure that the British public so loved.

Prior to his doomed effort on the Pole which, by only managing to reach 80 degrees 37 minutes, did not even challenge the previous record of 80 degrees 48 minutes, Franklin had achieved one success in slightly warmer climes. He had been with Matthew Flinders (*see* page 309) during his circumnavigation and mapping of Australia, a feat that had left all who had been involved highly regarded. In addition, little blame was attached to the Englishman for the bad luck, bad weather and bad preparation that had thwarted his North Pole attempt and so he remained near the top of the pecking order when a new approach to the Northwest Passage conundrum was considered by the Admiralty.

The plan was simple. While Parry led his first sea expedition into the Northwest Passage in 1819, Franklin would lead an overland party across northern Canada and begin tracking and mapping its coastline. In the process, the two parties would hopefully meet up, with Franklin using his new knowledge of the shores he had encountered to help guide Parry through the rest of the Passage.

It was a disaster from the start. Parry was already leading his second expedition to the Foxe Basin, in pursuit of the Passage, before Franklin had even made it to the north Canadian coastline. Although he had set out from England within two weeks of Parry's initial 1819 assault, it had then taken Franklin over a year just to make it to the perceived 'starting point' – a log cabin camp he established near the Coppermine River called Fort Enterprise – for his difficult onward journey. Furthermore, a full two years had passed since leaving Britain before the party actually set out from there in earnest for the North American shoreline.

Everything that could have gone wrong had gone wrong. The plan had been for Franklin's group, made up of only a small party of Britons, to obtain assistance and guidance from the men of the two dominant commercial enterprises in northern Canada at that time, the Hudson Bay Company and the North West Company. A fierce rivalry between the two businesses and a joint lack of interest in the goals of Franklin's mission only served to hamper the explorer's progress. Moreover, he was soon separated from most of his supplies by the traders, which were then never forwarded as promised.

Franklin amassed a group of Canadian porters through the two companies, who were supposed to assist his party. In many cases, though, they simply proved to be a further drain on his already inadequate resources. They were often divisive and unmotivated and they threatened to mutiny on a number of occasions. Franklin also hired a number of local men to hunt for and feed his team as the outfit moved into native Indian territory, but food was scarce and the Indians often struggled just to feed themselves. The local men were also meant to act as guides later in the journey but their knowledge of the land was largely found wanting and was little better than that of the British men.

Nevertheless, in June 1821, Franklin at last left Fort Enterprise for the Coppermine River, which he intended to follow to the Canadian coast. By July, they had entered

Eskimo territory. The Eskimos were the enemies of the Indians and so the local Indians left the party, taking with them their hunting skills and their doubtful guidance abilities. A few days later Franklin's party at last reached the sea. Twenty-one men remained in the party; six Englishmen, including Franklin, and fifteen Canadian porters. Over the next weeks they travelled eastwards in canoes, tracking over five hundred miles of shoreline until their supplies had all but run out. Not having encountered Parry (unsurprisingly, as by now he was locked in the Foxe Basin on his second mission, several hundred miles to the east), there was nothing for it but to turn back for Fort Enterprise, which Franklin had instructed the Indians to load up with supplies in case of just such an event.

The shortest route back was an uncharted trek overland, but they still had to carry canoes with them in order to cross any water encountered along the way. As it was now September, it was becoming colder and hunting successes were few and far between as the majority of wild animals migrated south. Gradually, the team disintegrated from hunger, weakness and discord. They became separated and began dumping equipment, including their last canoe. Only forty miles from Fort Enterprise they reached the Coppermine River again but could not cross it, losing more valuable days to starvation as a new vessel was constructed.

Finally having crossed the river, an advanced, stronger party was sent to make a dash for the Fort Enterprise supplies: weaker members had already started dying. They arrived in early October, only to find the fort was empty. The Indians, who had by now headed south for the winter, had believed Franklin's men would never return alive and so had left no supplies. Some members of the advanced party therefore moved on to try to catch up with the tribe, their only hope of salvation.

Meanwhile, the slower group had been split into two again. Those who could not go on had set up camp to await those who could still walk; including Franklin, who had pledged to complete a return trip to Fort Enterprise with supplies. Alas, Franklin's group were the next to realise that the fort was barren, at which point they collapsed in disappointment and fatigue.

By now, back at the camp of the desperate, one of the porters had secretly begun to resort to cannibalism. Three members of the group 'disappeared' before a fourth was openly shot and the man-eater himself could only be stopped with a bullet to the head. With no supplies arriving, the survivors eventually limped to Fort Enterprise.

Just as all hope seemed to be lost, with two of the party at Fort Enterprise also having passed away, some Indians returned with food in early November. The advanced men had at last caught up with them and a rescue mission had been mounted. The survivors were gradually nursed back to health. It would be the following year before the British men among them eventually made it back to their home country. They had been away for over three years, more than half the Coppermine River party had died and the expedition had barely achieved anything of worth. Yet Franklin, in his failure, had suffered like no other Northwest Passage adventurer before him. The British public loved him for it.

So popular in fact did Franklin's fiasco prove to be that he was soon sent out on a repeat mission. While the public and the Admiralty had not learned their lessons in their clamour for heroic victims, however, Franklin had. This time his preparations were meticulous and the whole affair was mundanely successful. He ensured that sufficient supplies were laid out in advance and that only appropriate and often specifically designed equipment was carried, based on his previous experiences. He also relied on outside parties as little as possible. The other main difference was that this time the party would travel along the Mackenzie River to the North American coast, further to the west than the Coppermine River. The expedition lasted from 1825 to 1827 and on arrival at the Canadian shoreline it was divided into two. One group successfully mapped the coastline between the Mackenzie and Coppermine rivers, the other a significant portion to the west, before returning to base camp.

The expedition had unravelled many of the mysteries of the North American coastline for any future vessel attempting to make its way out of the Northwest Passage. Yet in spite of repeated attempts by Parry and others, by 1845 no-one had found a channel through to this shoreline from the east. So it was that the Admiralty turned to Franklin again, who by now was nearly sixty.

His land travel days were over, but he was first and foremost an officer of the navy. Franklin, as much as any of his contemporaries, had always been keen to be the man to complete the sea Passage and at last he was given his chance. Sadly, it would be a disastrous undertaking for Franklin: one that would ensure his immortality and enduring popularity with the British public but also one that would cost him his life, together with those of all of the crews of the two ships.

For a long time, nobody really knew what had happened. When Franklin sailed off with the *Erebus* and the *Terror* in May 1845, fully equipped and with several years' provisions, the public expected him to return with a hard-luck tale at the very least. But once the ships had entered the depths of the Arctic they were never seen again. Back in Britain, everybody was initially so unconcerned that serious consideration was not given to a rescue mission until 1848. In the end, three expeditions were sent out without success and countless others followed in their wake over the next decade.

It was already too late. All that the salvage parties had managed to unearth were notes that had been left in cairns, detailing the demise of the expedition and, eventually, abandoned equipment and bodies. One message confirmed the death of Franklin on 11 June 1847 and the abandonment of both ships in the ice off King William Island in April 1848. Slowly, over the next couple of years, the remainder of the ships' crews had perished as they tried to walk to safety.

The Northwest Passage remained unconquered and had claimed even more victims, including the great, unfortunate Franklin. In the decade after his failure to return, his legend had never been more popular. Fame through misfortune had found a new level of frenzy.

Sir James Clark Ross *(1800–1862)*

Among the first rescue parties to go in search of Franklin in 1848 was one led by James Clark Ross. He had by this point already retired from Arctic life – indeed, he had previously turned down the chance to lead the doomed Franklin expedition on just such a basis – yet he did not hesitate to return to service on the realisation that his friend and colleague might need help. But then that was the kind of man James Ross was. Of all the early nineteenth century Arctic explorers, or Antarctic for that matter, he was the one who quite simply just got on with it. And usually succeeded.

Unfortunately, the Franklin rescue attempt was one occasion when even Ross struggled to make progress. Later rescue parties would eventually ascertain the fate of his compatriot's expedition. Ross would never go to the Arctic again, but by then he was already held in such high esteem that little could be done to damage his reputation. It had not always been so well established. For most of his career, James Ross had been very much the quiet achiever. He had joined the Navy at the age of just eleven, sailing under the stewardship of his uncle John Ross. He was also very much in his shadow, a place where he would remain for the majority of his professional life. While John Ross was a blustering, dominant veteran commander, quick to make enemies and impossible to ignore, James was the man who, for the most part, simply got on with his peers and subordinates alike, respected by all with the minimum of fuss.

While he was going largely unnoticed by the British public, James Ross was also quietly gathering such a body of knowledge about Arctic exploration – particularly regarding the tackling of the Northwest Passage – that he would eventually be unrivalled as the most experienced polar authority in the British navy. He sailed with his uncle on his controversial 1818 attempt on the Northwest Passage. Unlike John Ross, however, he continued to be held in high regard by all who had been with him on this voyage and Parry was keen to have him in his team for his own, much more successful, foray in the following year. It was the beginning of a long association between the two men: James Ross subsequently sailed on all of Parry's three attempts at the Passage and ventured with him overland on his 1827 quest for the North Pole. Moreover, he continued his Arctic and Antarctic career long after Parry had retired from the cause. It was no wonder that the Admiralty turned to James Ross as the man who might just be able to save Franklin, if any one could.

Furthermore, while Ross was impressively augmenting his *curriculum vitae* between 1818 and 1827, he was also establishing a reputation of unfussy competence for himself. He excelled in almost every task he was given. When an expedition was floundering, Ross was usually the man who found or achieved something from which it could claw back some credit. If the men had concerns or problems, they more often than not came to Ross first. If the captain or commander found himself in a position where he could not undertake a task for any reason, Ross was usually the one to whom he would turn in the safe knowledge that the action would be well accomplished.

Parry, for example, usually entrusted many of his daily official duties to Ross in his later expeditions, when he was frequently too unwell or weak to undertake them himself. Ross quietly became a second leader in the expeditions in which he took part, the backbone on which most attempts at an Arctic goal depended for its main hope of success. By the time they had completed their fourth expedition together, this time towards the Pole, Parry was in awe of the man who, when all others were flagging, kept them moving forever northwards towards their goal. He later wrote, 'To the islet off Little Table Island … the northernmost known land upon the globe, I have applied the name of Lieutenant Ross in the chart; for … no individual can have exerted himself more strenuously to rob it of that distinction.' It would not be the last time Ross's name would be given to landmarks in his honour.

The expedition in which Ross finally ascended a level in the public consciousness, however, was his uncle's resurgent and predominately ice-trapped attempt at the Northwest Passage between 1829 and 1833. It was a truly tortuous saga.

As was so often the case, the party's fortunes had

initially looked promising. On arriving in the Arctic aboard the *Victory* in the summer of 1829, John Ross was to learn that the weather during the navigable season was proving to be very mild indeed. Many of the usually ice-choked passages were, for once, open water. This was his chance. In August, he breezed into Prince Regent Inlet, soon sailing beyond the beach where Parry had been obliged to abandon the *Fury* and many of its supplies during his last attempt at the Northwest Passage in 1825. By September he was hundreds of miles further into the inlet than Parry had ever been able to achieve, desperately hoping there would be a channel that would allow him to slip past the western side of the land that he had named Boothia Felix. Sadly, the passage would not be forthcoming and, worst still, the winter ice moved in while they were in the depths of Prince Regent Inlet. It was never again to release the *Victory* in any useful capacity whilst Ross's men stayed aboard. They remained locked in the inlet for the next three years, only ever moving a few miles towards its exit during the brief summer seasons, before abandoning ship for good.

In the interim, however, James Ross had come into his own. He had used the ice-trapped time and the party's subsequent contact with passing Eskimos to master the difficult task of dog-sledging. This accomplished, during 1830 and 1831 he led countless exploratory missions across Boothia Felix and to a new landfall on the other side of the peninsula which he named King William Land (now Island). His crowning glory, however, was his discovery of the North Magnetic Pole on the west side of Boothia Felix at the head of a sledging expedition on 1 June 1831. With this feat alone, James Ross had achieved more than his over-arching uncle, who remained safely tucked up in his ship on the other side of the peninsula, had ever managed. Indeed, it would be one of the enduring exploits that would ensure the elevation and maintenance of James Ross's profile when the crew eventually made it back to Britain.

This escape also ultimately relied heavily on the stamina of James Ross. By 1832, his uncle had decided to abandon ship and drag its smaller boats overland to the site of the *Fury*'s plentiful supplies, several hundred miles further up the coast. When progress was slow and supplies were running low, however, because of the time it was taking to haul the unwieldy boats with them, it was James Ross who came to their aid again. He completed a 300-mile round-trip 'dash' ahead to confirm that the *Fury*'s own small boats were still in place and the stores were accessible, such that the remaining crew could abandon their own boat-dragging activities and sprint with him back to Fury Beach.

Even from their new position, however, they failed to escape Prince Regent Inlet that summer. In the following year, though, the waters finally opened sufficiently for them to sail and row their way out of their erstwhile trap and into Lancaster Sound, where they were eventually rescued by a passing British ship. During this gruelling period, James Ross's strength and leadership were again a vital component of their eventual salvation.

Still he was not finished with the ice. In 1836, James Ross returned to the Arctic at the head of a mission to rescue the crew of a distressed whaling ship. Three years later, he set off on a mammoth expedition to the other end of the world, where he would cement his name among the great explorers. Although following slightly behind both Jules d'Urville and Charles Wilkes (*see* page 261), Ross surpassed their achievements in an expedition to the region which, between winter stopovers at Tasmania and the Falklands, lasted four years.

During that time, as well as leading a series of important scientific observations on magnetism in the southern hemisphere, he had come close to the site of the South Magnetic Pole, being thwarted only a hundred miles or so from what would have been the completion of a remarkable double. He penetrated the Antarctic ice pack to unveil uncharted waters that became known as the Ross Sea. While in this area, he discovered the live volcano Mount Erebus, numerous islands off the Antarctic continent which he claimed in the name of Britain and the massive and impenetrable barrier of ice that was later named the Ross Ice Shelf. In 1842 he also set a new record by reaching a latitude of 78 degrees 11 minutes, the furthest anyone had ever gone south.

James Ross returned to England in 1843, having decided at last to hang up his ice-filled boots. Apart from the Franklin rescue attempt a few years later, it was a pledge that he would keep. Of all the British navy's early nineteenth century Northwest Passage explorers, Ross had certainly seen, and arguably achieved, more than any other.

Yet even the indomitable Sir James Ross had not been able to conquer the stubborn Passage itself. More than half a century was yet to elapse before anyone succeeded, the culmination of a four-hundred-year odyssey of, ultimately, no consequence whatsoever.

Chapter 7

FURTHEST NORTH:

The Quest for the North Pole

If the quest for the Northwest Passage had increasingly become a story of almost tragically comic proportions, then the pursuit of the North Pole soon surpassed it for adventure, morbid humour and, above all, drama. The quest for the top of the world captured the imagination of explorers and the public like no other, and by the mid-nineteenth century, the race was on in earnest.

Fittingly, it had been the men whose names are most associated with the Northwest Passage who had also kicked off the search for the North Pole. John Franklin had been a member of the David Buchan attempt in 1818. William Parry had achieved a new furthest north record during his 1827 stab, that stood for nearly half a century. Unwittingly, Franklin then sparked a new race for the Pole with the disappearance of the expedition that had left Britain in pursuit of the Passage in 1845. Countless 'rescue' searches were launched, some earnestly so and others that simply, and increasingly, became disguised attempts to establish a route to the North Pole. Significantly, Britain was not the only country that joined in the search for Franklin which, for the first time, notably included Arctic parties sent out by the United States.

The authorities in Britain, meanwhile, were growing increasingly sick of the expense and loss being incurred in the Arctic. In time, Britain would virtually drop out of the region altogether. Certainly, when the new race began the only real British expedition in pursuit of the Pole was that under Captain George Nares between 1875 and 1876. This attempt finally bettered Parry's earlier northern latitude record, but still came nowhere near the Pole. Franz Josef Land surveyor Frederick Jackson also tried briefly again for Britain from 1896 to 1897, but he barely got started before he had to admit defeat.

In 1968–69, in some respects, Britain achieved a final Arctic epitaph for the race it had initiated more than a hundred and fifty years before. This was when Wally Herbert, a British explorer, completed the first undisputed expedition on foot to the North Pole. Not content with that alone, he then carried on to walk across the entire Arctic ice pack. But by then, the real race for the North Pole, in any meaningful sense of the word, was long since over. And, as it reached its conclusion, it would increasingly be a competition between the United States and Scandinavia.

Not that representatives from other nations had also neglected to launch their own bids along the way. Russia, in Herbertesque fashion, retains her own claim to the Pole with the first agents to unquestionably set foot on top of the world, after they had flown there in 1948. Previously, when it was still not clear if the race for the Pole was actually over or not, she had also launched a far less successful expedition under Gregoriy Sedov in

1913–14. Earlier still, Germany had made her attempt (1869–70), then Austria–Hungary (1872–74) and, most notably, Italy (1899–1900) under the Duke of Abruzzi, which achieved a then new furthest north record of 86 degrees 33 minutes latitude.

The means by which people attempted to transport themselves to the Pole also grew increasingly adventurous, even at times verging on the comedic, if the human losses that so often followed in their wake had not occurred. Britain at first thought that it was possible to sail there (under Buchan and Franklin) then man-sledge (Parry). Many others also attempted to use the same methods. Later dog-sledging, rightly, came into fashion. Along the way, though, there were hot-air balloon attempts, aeroplane forays, airship sorties and even submarine plots, some enjoying a greater degree of success than others.

Yet in spite of all this equipment, expense and loss of life and limb over decades of Arctic exploration, no-one really knows who won or even what mode of transport was used. Robert Peary and his dog-sledging team are usually credited with the ultimate achievement in 1909, yet many dispute whether he really made it. Richard

Byrd supposedly took his aeroplane over the Pole in 1926 but others question his readings too.

Lincoln Ellsworth and Roald Amundsen definitely did fly over the top of the world in their airship in 1926, but even they did not set foot on the Pole. Nonetheless, nobody disputed their claim and in a way it is perhaps the most fitting of all. For as a combined American (Ellsworth) and Norwegian (Amundsen) expedition, it jointly represented the two nations that had arguably gone to the greatest lengths to win the race to conquer the North Pole.

Elisha Kent Kane *(1820–1857)*

If a single man could be said to have been responsible for dragging the United States into the race for the North Pole, then that person would almost certainly have to be Elisha Kent Kane. By the standards of the later polar explorers, even by the standards of some of the earlier ones, he was not necessarily the most successful of adventurers. He was, however, a person with an uncanny knack for generating a gripping Arctic story and he possessed an even better talent for telling it such that the world could not ignore him.

Until the time of Franklin's disappearance in search of the Northwest Passage in 1845, the United States had had no real opportunity, or at least no real excuse, to head into the Arctic. With the British explorer's mysterious vanishing act, however, the perfect opportunity presented itself. The United States was located nearer than most to the likely site of the Franklin party after all. Moreover, the public there were just as fascinated by, and cared almost as much about, his exploits as those back in Britain. The USA had a duty to join in the search. Or at least that was the opinion of certain key individuals with rather deep pockets.

Henry Grinnell was one such wealthy man. Unlike Britain with her Northwest Passage forays, the United States had no history of state sponsored expeditions to the north. Consequently, when its citizens did finally become involved in the polar region, it was normally on the basis of a few motivated individuals who eventually brought the rest of the country along with them. Henry Grinnell certainly had the motivation to spend his money on sending others to the Arctic and Elisha Kane certainly had the motivation to take advantage of it and bring everyone else, metaphorically if not physically, along for the ride.

So it was that, in 1850, the first Grinnell-funded expedition to join in the Franklin search was launched. America, albeit privately, was at last in the Arctic race and Elisha Kane was its medical officer. But that would not be enough. When the party returned a year later with, as was typically the case, only limited information as to the fate of Franklin's men, Kane was soon knocking on Grinnell's door: not only did he want to be sent back to the Arctic, but this time he wanted to lead the expedition himself.

Although Kane had joined the American navy, he was never much of a seaman and had virtually no qualifications to head such a mission. After all, he was first and foremost a physician. He had done his chances no harm, however, by generating a huge amount of publicity around the first expedition on its return which, coincidentally of course, happened to throw his name into the spotlight. Kane was a great speaker and a mesmerising writer and, almost single-handedly, he gripped the nation into demanding more Arctic enterprises. So Grinnell opened his chequebook, Kane loaded his boat and all of America was proud.

Kane departed on the *Advance* in May 1853, with a small crew of just seventeen which was later augmented with two Greenlanders who were making their way north. By this time he had become 'convinced' that Franklin must be trapped to the north of where the rescue missions had so far looked. His guess was the 'Open Polar Sea', a then popular notion that suggested a clear body of water that surrounded the Pole and its environs. There was in fact little evidence for either the sea or the fact that Franklin had attempted to go there, but the expedition, in name at least, was still meant to be a rescue mission. By heading due north up Smith Sound, however, the place where it was believed that such an entrance to the Open Polar Sea could be found, an attempt on the North Pole conveniently became a possibility.

Fittingly, perhaps, the mission proved almost 'Franklinesque' in its trials from start to finish. It was under-provisioned from the beginning. Fuel for heating and cooking soon ran low and fresh food, other than the limited amount they could catch, was almost non-existent from the outset, as were other vitals required for staving off scurvy. The dogs Kane had bought for the purpose of sledge-hauling nearly all died from a sudden illness. Meanwhile, the crew was largely inexperienced in polar conditions. Some of the men frequently fought amongst themselves and many of them were soon questioning and undermining Kane's leadership. Indeed, the threat of mutiny hung over the whole expedition from the outset.

Nevertheless, up Smith Sound Kane merrily bobbed, happy just to be leading his men, and to all intents and purposes his country, on the grand kind of adventure he had always craved. He had soon sailed further into Smith Sound than any expedition before him, which already ensured him a degree of immortality. His next aim, spoken or unspoken, was to take Parry's overall furthest north record for his country. If he were to achieve this, however, it would need to be done by sledge as, by September, he was firmly iced into a winter mooring on the northwest Greenland coast that he called Rensselaer Harbour. The early omens were good, though; one autumn reconnaissance effort unveiled the mammoth Humboldt Glacier, the biggest in the Arctic, another important achievement for which Kane's expedition would be remembered.

During the winter months, however, events took a downturn. The supply shortages soon became apparent, no more so than when members of the crew already began to show signs of scurvy. Kane then sent some of these weakened men out on a preparatory sledging mission too early in the new year, with the consequence that another group had to be sent out to rescue them. Both parties returned in a dilapidated state, several of the men suffering from frostbite and having to have toes or whole feet amputated. Two of them died shortly afterwards from related complications or infections. Later sledging forays in April and May proved equally futile, with Kane himself one of the worst affected this time.

Summer came and although the fresh meat it brought in the form of northward migrating animals helped their scurvy, the *Advance* showed no signs of breaking free from the ice. While they waited, however, two members of Kane's team racked up the additional success he so desperately needed to justify the sacrifices they had already incurred. They discovered, or so they erroneously believed, the Open Polar Sea. The men, named Hendrik and Morton, had penetrated beyond the 81st parallel and up the coast of Greenland, further north than any others in the party had so far managed. Here the land had opened up into a large, flowing expanse of sea, 'proof' of Kane's most important polar belief. Unfortunately, as later explorers would discover, the crewmen had merely seen a local body of water that happened to be open at that moment and a mirage beyond.

Kane would like to have explored it further or, failing that, return to report the news of his discovery, but he could not: his ship barely moved during the summer. He attempted to drag and then sail a boat south to obtain more supplies, but the party was firmly trapped in Smith Sound.

As the autumn approached again, with no prospect of their release that year, supplies almost run out and scurvy was abundant. Kane gave his men the option to make a break southwards if they so chose. He intended to stay and see out the worst, but half the men decided to leave, an act he considered nothing short of mutinous even though he had brought up the idea. Among them was Isaac Israel Hayes, who would later lead his own expedition in search of the Pole. At this particular point in time, though, it was not certain that he would ever return alive to even contemplate such a prospect.

The breakaway party's fortunes certainly proved no better than the situation of those left on the ship. They made some progress and obtained some fresh meat from the Eskimos before having to concede defeat to the elements and damaged boats and bedded down into temporary shelter for the winter. Slowly they began to starve, eventually coming to fear the Eskimos themselves as scavengers who would either kill them in their weakened state, or just wait for them to die anyway, so they could avail themselves of the explorers' equipment. In desperation, then, they compelled the Eskimos at gunpoint to sledge them back to the *Advance* where those who had remained were just as forlorn. Kane allowed the 'deserters' aboard, but only grudgingly.

Somehow they survived the winter, starving and almost all suffering from scurvy, with three more individual attempts at desertion, one ultimately successful, until the spring game arrived. At last there was enough to eat to restore their strength and cure their ills. Still, though, there was no sign that their vessel would be freed by the ice, so finally Kane decided that the whole party should abandon ship. In May 1855 they left the *Advance*, dragging their boats and supplies, and headed south until, at last, they reached open water. The journey had not been without incident, though, for another member of the party had died in an accident along the way.

Starving, the remaining crew members rowed and sailed ever southwards until, thankfully, they were rescued by a whaling ship in August. They were taken back to a port in Greenland called Upernavik, where eventually they were picked up by a US rescue ship that had been sent to try to find the missing expedition.

When they arrived back in New York shortly afterwards, Kane was received as an all-conquering hero. Most of the party had returned alive, they had survived unthinkable hardships, they had penetrated further up Smith Sound than any before and, what was more, they had discovered the Open Polar Sea. The journal of Kane's first expedition in 1854 had already proved a bestseller and the new account of his latest travels, published under the title *Arctic Explorations* in 1856, leapt off the shelves even more rapidly. Thanks to Kane, Americans were now as interested in Arctic exploration as anyone else. Furthermore, he had ignited a new desire to investigate this Open Polar Sea and, ultimately, the North Pole that stood unconquered within it.

But Kane would not be the one to do the exploring. He had always suffered from bad health anyway, but his long ordeal, followed by the pressure of preparing his journal for speedy publication, had damaged his wellbeing beyond repair. After a tour to England in 1856 followed by a voyage to Cuba in early 1857 to convalesce, he succumbed to his illnesses at the age of just thirty-seven.

Instead, it was Hayes who picked up the baton with an 1860 expedition up Smith Sound. Again, it was a private affair with Grinnell proving once more the major sponsor. Amazingly, Hayes too returned with further sightings of the Open Polar Sea to underline Kane's earlier findings. Less surprisingly, he too arrived home with a tale of hardship. Again, the dogs had died. A mission sent to retrieve some more had resulted in the death of one of its members and his ship had been so badly damaged during the voyage that he had been forced to abandon plans to proceed farther north. He limped home, barely managing to stay afloat.

Now famous American names lined up for their chance to dance with the Pole and, more realistically, death, as they tried to outdo each other with tortuous tales on the odd occasions on which they actually managed to return. Charles Francis Hall undertook three expeditions to the Arctic between 1860 and 1871. He spent long periods living with Eskimos during the first two in an attempt to learn the survival techniques that he believed would prove to be the key to polar success. On the third expedition he penetrated Smith Sound farther north than any other (then died, probably murdered by his own men). George Washington De Long had a go through the Bering Strait between 1879 and 1882 (starved to death along with many of his men: twenty out of the thirty-three in the party died). Adolphus Greeley's team achieved a new northern latitude record of 83 degrees 24 minutes from Ellesmere Island during an 1881–84 mission (eighteen of the twenty-four-strong party perished from starvation).

No matter, just like the British people had been during their countrymen's trials in the Northwest Passage, the American public were hooked on the grisly reports of polar folly. Regardless of how badly events unfolded, the Arctic explorers were heroes; the more disastrously things went wrong, the more enthralling and morbidly fascinating the journal. Moreover, by the late 1880s, in Robert Edwin Peary they had a man emerging at last who, after having endured enough suffering and hardship to earn his spurs, might just be able to reach the Pole.

That was if the Scandinavians did not beat him to it first.

Fridtjof Nansen *(1861–1930)*

In the 1870s and 1880s, the then united territory of Sweden–Norway had at last come of age as an Arctic exploration force. Its geographical location made it an obvious candidate and plenty of its inhabitants had cold-weather and water experience in the form of whaling, hunting and other commercial enterprises, but it was only at this time that Scandinavian explorers fully joined the race. The first true indication of what could be achieved came with the traversing of the Northeast Passage by the Swede Nordenskjöld between 1878 and 1879 (*see* page 54). Next, the Norwegian, Fridtjof Nansen stepped up with an almost effortless crossing of Greenland from east to west in 1888, the first of its kind. It was merely a signal of Nansen's intent. The Greenland adventure would be just a warm-up for the goal he truly prized, the North Pole.

It was not always meant to have been this way for Nansen, however. He had spent his early life in academia, studying for what looked to be a promising career in neurology. Like so many others before him, though, he had caught the polar bug and there was no shaking it off. Instead, he would become an explorer. 'Man wants to know', he said, 'and when he ceases to do so, he is no longer a man.' After the Greenland expedition brought him fame and wide popularity within Norway, a return to his former quiet life was even more out of the question. The only matter remaining was which Pole, or at least which should be first, North or South? Nansen chose the North.

One of Nansen's great strengths as an explorer was his ability to think 'outside of the box': to do things differently. It was this that led him to contemplate the idea of using the currents that moved within the Arctic ice pack to literally carry him to the Pole. To do this, he would need a vessel that could withstand the huge pressures involved in such a passage. This resulted in him dreaming up the idea of the *Fram*, a purpose-built boat that was designed in such a way that it would not be crushed or nipped by the ice. Nansen's other key competitive advantage over most of his rivals was that he was an excellent skier. His Greenland success had been achieved on the back of this skill; his subsequent polar achievements would also rely heavily on this method.

All he needed for a serious attempt on the Pole, therefore, was the finance to put his vision in place.

Leaning on his fame, he appealed to the Norwegian people and hierarchy, and the growing sense of nationalism that would eventually result in an independent Norway, to obtain the funds he needed. This achieved, he worked closely with a Scottish ship designer and builder called Colin Archer to produce the revolutionary *Fram*. It would not disappoint and subsequent experience in the ice would prove that it worked exactly as designed, floating upwards out of its claws whenever the frozen water tried to nip the vessel.

All of the arrangements in place then, Nansen set out from what is now the city of Oslo (then called Christiana) in June 1893. He had a small crew of only twelve with him for what would prove to be a three-year odyssey in the ice. Together they journeyed around the upper tip of Norway and along the northern Russian coastline as far as Siberia before heading due north towards the Pole and straight into the Arctic ice pack. From here, Nansen hoped the *Fram* would slowly be pulled across the top of the world by the shifting currents.

Sadly, they were too shifting. Sometimes he was pulled toward the Pole, but just as frequently he was dragged south again, or to the east or the west. For two winters the crew simply sat in the *Fram* waiting for something to happen, hoping that one of the ever-changing currents would eventually carry them to their goal. Such a momentum did not arrive. Worse still, Nansen himself proved to be far from the easiest commander to serve under and at certain moments not a little arrogant, such that as time wore on everybody began bickering.

After two years of discontent and boredom, they had all had enough, not least Nansen himself. It was time for action. Having made preparations during the previous months for just such an event, Nansen decided it was the moment to resort to the skis again. He and a colleague from the *Fram* called Hjalmar Johanssen would ski their way to the Pole in as fast a manner as possible, with a team of dogs pulling sledges containing supplies, before returning to Franz Jozef Land or Spitsbergen where they would hope to hail a lift home on a passing ship. The leadership of the *Fram* would pass to Nansen's deputy, Otto Sverdrup, who later went on to complete important exploratory and mapping surveys off Ellesmere Island between 1898 and 1902. First, however he had to steer the *Fram* home, just as soon as the ice released her. This finally came about after another winter had been spent embedded within it in August 1896. By this time, there was still no news back in Norway of Nansen's fate. It would only be literally a matter of days, however, before the full details emerged.

Nansen and Johanssen had left the *Fram* in March 1895. By April they had achieved a new furthest north record of 86 degrees 13 minutes. This, however, would only be the beginning of an epic journey that was to last for more than a year. Running low on supplies and being pushed southwards at an unsustainable rate by the ice pack, Nansen realised at this point that he could not achieve the Pole and would have to head back. So, their new best achieved, they turned around for what they hoped would be a relatively straightforward journey back to Franz Josef Land.

It was not. The same shifting currents that had given them so much frustration aboard the *Fram* now endeavoured to do the same to the two men on skis. Whichever direction they headed in, the ice pack contrived to drag them the other way. Even more seriously, their watches stopped for a period, which meant that they were left having to estimate their longitude so they risked missing their destination altogether. In July, however, they sighted land and by August they had landed upon it. They could not be certain that it was one of the many islands of the Franz Josef Land archipelago and, even if it was, that they would ever be rescued from such a remote location. With no sign of life in the immediate vicinity, therefore, they continued to head southwards.

Kayaking by now, they reached another small island by the end of the month but, as the sea began to freeze again and the conditions worsened, realised they were going to have to spend another winter in the Arctic. Their only salvation was that they had been able to shoot plenty of wildlife during their voyage to sustain them through this period, so they set up a temporary shelter and waited. In May 1896, the explorers set off southwards in their canoes again until, a month later, following an attack by walruses, they were forced to stop on another stretch of land for several days to make repairs.

Amazingly, and unknown to Nansen, a British scientific expedition had based itself nearby under a man named Frederick Jackson, where it had been spending the last couple of years charting the hitherto sketchy geographical details of Franz Josef Land. By a complete coincidence the two parties crossed each other's paths and Nansen and Johanssen were rescued. The British party had built a shelter of sturdy huts and had regular supplies brought to them by ship, so they had plenty of food and other luxuries to go round. The supply ship arrived in July and it took the two Scandinavians with it when it departed again in August, just as the *Fram* itself was at last en route to Norway. The British, however, were left behind to continue their survey. Indeed, Jackson was so inspired by Nansen's story that he even briefly attempted to launch his own stab at the Pole from his advantageous starting point of Franz Josef Land, but it quickly came to nothing.

Nansen and Johanssen, and the crew of the *Fram*, meanwhile, were received as all-conquering heroes. They might not have made the Pole, but they had smashed the furthest north record and, in a rare Arctic foray, everybody had survived. Although Nansen would never again attempt the conquest of the north, or indeed Antarctica's Pole in the south as he had anticipated, he would become a mentor to future Scandinavian explorers and would be forever celebrated as one of the Arctic greats.

In the aftermath of Nansen's return, the only event that looked as if it might take the shine off his triumph was the distinct possibility that another Scandinavian might almost immediately steal his record. This time it was a Swede, by the name of Salomon Andrée who had come up with the idea of hot-air ballooning to the Pole. Initially ridiculed for the proposition, people realised that he was deadly serious when he brought together the necessary equipment and a crew in Spitsbergen in the summer of 1896. Weather conditions did not prove to be conducive to making the attempt that year, but he was back the following summer. He set off with his two colleagues, Knut Fraenkel and Nils Strindberg in July 1897. If all went to plan he was anticipated to reach the Pole and beyond within a mere matter of days. In spite of a difficult initial ascent, early indications – brought to the outside world in the form of a note strapped to a homing pigeon – showed that all was going well. The message said that they had passed the 82nd parallel; everything was proceeding according to plan. They were never heard from again.

It would not be until 1930 that the truth of what had happened eventually emerged, when the remains of three bodies and Andrée's journals were found off White Island, near Spitsbergen. The weather had turned and had forced the balloon down a long way short of even Nansen's northerly record. Anticipating such an eventuality the explorers had brought overland equipment with them and they began the long, and ultimately forlorn, trek back to their starting point. Probably through disease, they had perished short of their target and with their deaths went their still high hopes of another balloon attempt on the Pole which, had they been more fortunate, might well have seen them win the race in subsequent years. Such was the fine line between success and failure, life and death, in the world of exploration.

Nevertheless, Sweden–Norway was now firmly leading the way in the race for the Pole. Nansen and Andrée had shown the world that the Northern European state was a serious contender and the wave of enthusiasm they had unleashed in their homeland was expected to inspire more attempts in the near future.

By the end of the nineteenth century, only one outsider looked as if he could possibly thwart the Scandinavians. He was the American Robert Edwin Peary and he firmly believed that the North Pole did, in fact, belong to him and him alone.

Robert Edwin Peary *(1856–1920)*

Robert Edwin Peary had certainly been busy racking up polar experience. By the turn of the new century he was already famous as a leading Arctic explorer and polar authority. Yet, as with the Scandinavians and his American predecessors, the North Pole continued to elude him also. In truth, at this point in time he had still arrived nowhere near it. And although, after much controversy, he would later be credited as the man who arrived at the Pole first, there remains doubt as to whether he ever even reached his goal at all.

In a way, though, Peary lived for controversy as much as he lived to reach the Pole. He certainly revelled in the huge amount of media coverage that followed his every expedition, bringing his profile to an ever wider audience. He had lusted after fame and immortality from a young age and, in many respects, he did not care how he achieved it, as long as he did.

As a child Peary had been gripped by the journals of Kane, but when he later settled on the idea of exploration as a route to recognition, it was initially with a view to warmer climes. Like Kane he joined the navy as a base from which to establish himself and like Kane he was largely dissatisfied with life within the service, at least until he was posted to Nicaragua. Here he thought that he might be able to make his mark as an explorer. He certainly enjoyed his time there and it proved a sound physical training ground for his later exploits, but it was not, ultimately, a route to stardom. So again, Peary began casting around for ideas and, in 1885, he landed upon the notion of Arctic exploration. In this domain there remained a vast expanse of uncharted territory, not to mention the Pole itself, in which Peary could make his mark. His mind was made up: this would be his world, a conviction he held with increasing obsession as he delved further into its depths.

In 1886, he undertook his first mission with the aim of crossing Greenland. There remained many questions about the lie of its inland territory and Peary decided that he was the man to resolve them. He set off two years before Nansen's later attempt at the same goal but, unlike the Scandinavian, Peary's expedition was far from successful. He was soon forced to turn back, hundreds of miles from the attainment of his target. Although he salvaged what he could from the expedition's feats in an effort to boost his reputation on returning to America, he was still far from the high-profile success he aspired to be.

Something grander needed to be achieved, particulary after Nansen had usurped him in crossing Greenland in 1888. This time, therefore, Peary would travel to its northernmost point, proving once and for all that the land mass stopped short of the North Pole itself. He set out in the summer of 1891. In spite of breaking his leg early in the voyage, after which he made an initial winter stop to recover, on the west Greenland coast at the southern end of Smith Sound, this expedition proved to be much more successful. Ironically, its main perceived achievement, the supposed discovery of Greenland's northernmost point, at a place Peary called Independence Bay, was a false one. It was later realised that this was not its location at all and, equally, the channel and separate mass of land Peary thought he saw ahead of him to the north of Greenland did not even exist. But Peary and a colleague called Eivind Astrup (ironically, a Norwegian) had, in that spring and summer of 1892, accomplished an unprecedented and speedy sledge round trip of more than 1,000 miles across Greenland. At last Peary returned to the fame he had desired for so long, a nationwide lecture tour in the wake of his mission's success further boosting his profile.

The 1891–92 expedition was also particularly notable because of two of the other participants who had accompanied Peary to the base from which he set off on his sledging journey. The first was Frederick Cook, a man who would later achieve his own place in the history of the North Pole race in an even more controversial fashion than Peary. The other was Matthew Henson, an employee of Peary's of African-American descent, who would subsequently accompany him on all of his additional polar adventures, becoming an accomplished explorer in his own right.

Thus, Henson joined Peary for his next stab at the north between 1893 and 1895, while Cook chose instead to pursue his own notorious career as an independent explorer. Peary's goal this time was at last the North Pole. On this occasion, though, he would get nowhere near it; indeed he would not even better his 1891–92 exploits. He spent the first year unsuccessfully trying to lay out a chain of supply depots for the northward march, after which most of the expeditionary party chose to return home on a supply ship. Only Peary, Henson and one other were left in Greenland, along with a support team of Eskimos, for the dash northwards in the spring of 1895. They just managed to reach Independence Bay again, but did not venture beyond. The only perceived 'success' of the voyage, beyond what had already been known, was in Peary's 'discovery' of three lumps of a meteorite that the local Eskimos had used as their only source of iron for generations. He promptly took possession of them, bringing two of the rocks home immediately and the other on a later voyage. For 'scientific' purposes he also brought six live Eskimos back with him, as well as several dead ones in the form of exhumed corpses.

This contentious behaviour aside, Peary's experience in the Arctic had made him appreciate the methods the Eskimos employed for survival in its harsh environment. Like his earlier compatriot, Charles Hall, he realised that they were the key to polar success. Consequently, he befriended them and adopted many of their techniques, as well as their clothing, for his northern forays. Henson in particular excelled in this area and in his mastery of the Eskimo language. Peary increasingly used Eskimos on his actual expeditions too, and the four long years he spent on his next Arctic trip were no exception.

In spite of this, however, the 1898 to 1902 mission in many ways became Peary's nadir as an explorer. It started badly. Peary lost eight of his toes to frostbite on a foolhardy sledging mission to Fort Conger, on Ellesmere Island in the winter of 1898. He had been 'forced' into such an action because he had believed that Otto Sverdrup, who was in the region undertaking his geographical surveys (and had no designs on the Pole whatsoever), was secretly planning an attempt on the Pole ahead of him.

The middle period passed no better. Ellesmere Island initially proved to be no more successful a launch pad for the Pole than Greenland, contrary to Peary's hopes, not least because his feet had still not healed properly and he struggled to walk. And it ended badly. Peary had believed that a 1902 ascent from Ellesmere Island had attained a new northerly record of 84 degrees 17 minutes for an expedition that had set out from a land base rather than a ship. However, it was revealed that this record had been comprehensively smashed in 1900 by an Italian expedition under the Duke of Abruzzi. The only other consolation for Peary was that in 1900, on another foray northwards, he had finally reached Greenland's actual northernmost point: but this only underlined the error he had made on his earlier expedition.

Still, however, the man refused to be beaten. He returned home and, in spite of waning public interest and a decline in his own credibility, he could not rest idle for long. By 1905, now approaching the age of fifty, he was back. This time there would be no messing around: he would use his newly-built 'ice-ship' the *Roosevelt* to obtain as high an initial altitude up the Smith Sound as possible and from there he would dart for the pole. He did well before having to bed in for the winter, penetrating to a latitude that lay towards the very north of Ellesmere Island. When the weather began improving again in early 1906, Peary's small team from America, supplemented by more than fifty Eskimos, began undertaking sledging missions to set up food depots further north, to be used in the sprint for the Pole.

In March, he and Henson and several Eskimos set out for the top of the world. They did not make it. Progress was slower than hoped for and it soon became clear that they could not reach the Pole in the time they had available. Peary had to make do with a new furthest north record of 87 degrees 6 minutes instead. It was an achievement, but it was not the Pole and, worst still, people began to openly question his readings and his claims of the distances he had covered in the timescales he maintained, such that even the new record was brought into doubt. Sadly for Peary's reputation, this would not be the last time such accusations dogged him.

In 1908–1909 he tried again for one last time. Once more the *Roosevelt* successfully made it to the same latitude up Smith Sound. During the winter a new depot of sledge-hauled supplies nearly a hundred miles further north was established, from which Peary would launch his attempt in the spring. In late February, the first of the advance support teams set out and, in early March, Peary himself followed. Although conditions were not good early in the journey, they improved and so did the expedition's progress. By the beginning of April they were only approximately 130 miles from the Pole and at last it seemed within reach.

At this point, however, the controversy once again began. Peary told the captain of the *Roosevelt*, Robert Bartlett, who had only agreed to join this (and the previous, for that matter) mission on the condition that he could also accompany the final sledging party to the

Pole, that he would not in fact be allowed to join him for the last ascent. Only Henson and four Eskimos would escort Peary to the Pole. Conveniently, none of these, unlike Bartlett, knew how to use the instruments that would verify the point at which the team had reached the top of the world. Peary, therefore, had put himself in a position where he would be the only one who could verify their success.

And, indeed, success he achieved, claiming to have covered the final 130 miles in the astonishing (and hitherto unheard of) time of just four days. The return journey over the same ground was even swifter – a little over two! Peary and Henson had made 'the Pole at last' on 6 April 1909, but it was merely the beginning of a debate that still rages as to whether they could possibly have reached their target in the timescales claimed. The experience of subsequent explorers, such as Wally Herbert, and analyses based on scientific evidence and calculations suggests that they probably did not.

Yet the controversy over the truth of those last miles would be nothing compared to that which awaited Peary on his return to America. For in the meantime, his former polar companion, Frederick Cook, had emerged from a rival expedition to the north suggesting that he too had in fact reached the North Pole. What is more, he had beaten Peary to the prize by nearly a full year! The autumn of 1909 saw a media frenzy unlike any other as the two men exchanged blows and counterclaims in the public relations battle to have their achievements validated. Both men were hailed by different sections of the media and society as being both true victors and frauds. Initially, Cook, who had also benefited from being the first to break his story, was in the ascendancy. But as time passed, the Peary charm offensive moved into full swing and Cook in turn struggled to produce the believable documentation that would underline his achievement and which he had said was 'imminent'. The pendulum turned the other way and in due course Cook was 'proven' to be a fraudster and Peary, conversely, was 'proven' to be the true first explorer to the Pole. Certainly Cook's account and his lack of evidence made his the least likely story of the two, but the sad truth is quite possibly that neither of the men ever made it to the North Pole at all. Equally true is the fact that the world will probably never know for certain.

All that is known for sure is that Peary and his team

came very, very close. As an example of perseverance and dedication to his cause, few in the history of exploration rival Peary. As a pioneer of Arctic exploration, he is without doubt among the greats.

Richard Evelyn Byrd *(1888–1957)*

So if neither Peary nor Cook saw the Pole, then who was the first? One of the next credible claimants was Richard Evelyn Byrd. Almost predictably, however, his achievements have since been brought into question too!

The year 1926 saw another mini-race for the Pole unfold. With some uncertainty surrrounding Peary's feats, there remained the possibility that a new venture to the top of the world might in time be recognised as the first. Even if that turned out not to be the case, there were still plenty of scientific and geographical questions outstanding concerning the Arctic, not least whether any undiscovered land masses remained in the polar region. One of the quickest and easiest ways of answering all of these unknowns seemed to be by air. Thousands of square miles could be surveyed effortlessly from a bird's-eye position, certainly compared to the cumbersome and difficult task of ground exploration. Moreover it could achieve in days, even hours, what otherwise might take years to unveil.

So it was in the air that the new polar race began, with the pitting of aeroplane against airship. The former was undoubtedly quicker, but almost certainly less reliable, and was particularly prone to mechanical failure in the harsh Arctic climate. The latter was slower and also had some risk of explosion attached to it, but generally was more stable and consumed fuel at a slower rate. In 1926, Richard Evelyn Byrd, along with his American compatriot Floyd Bennett, chose the plane option. His competitors were the indefatigable Norwegian Roald Amundsen (*see* page 291) and his American patron and colleague Lincoln Ellsworth.

Amundsen and Ellsworth had landed on the airship option after hard experience had taught them a year earlier of the pitfalls of the alternative. They had tried to fly to the Pole in two seaplanes, but one of them had developed engine trouble and they had been forced to land just north of the 87th parallel. After more than three weeks of carving a fluid airstrip in the ice, and with supplies running low, they finally managed to escape the Arctic in their one remaining plane. Next time, they decided, they would take the airship.

Richard Byrd, however, was having none of it. Born in Virginia in 1888, he was a man of the modern age, a confident pilot and a pioneer who was determined to stretch the bounds of plane travel. He had been at the forefront of America's aeronautical experimentation during World War I and had implicit faith in his planes. Much of his later reputation would be built on the back of air exploration in the Antarctic, where he played a prominent role in establishing America's revived interest in the region from 1928, but it would be in the North Pole that his early interest lay.

When Byrd arrived at Spitsbergen at the end of April 1926, from where he planned to launch his attempt, Amundsen and Ellsworth were already there. The Norwegian and his sponsor, along with their Italian pilot Umberto Nobile, were busy making preparations for the departure of their airship the *Norge*. They were still not ready, however, and would not be ready by the time Byrd and Bennett had unloaded their Fokker, tested it and subsequently taken off for the Pole on May 8. All the rival airship team could do was watch Byrd's plane disappear over the horizon and wait.

Apart from bone-chilling exposure to the elements and

an oil leak in one engine, the flight to the Pole passed in a relatively straightforward manner compared to the epic and arduous decades of land and sea expeditions that had gone before it. According to Byrd's account, they reached what they believed to be the Pole, turned around and found their way back to Spitsbergen in a round trip total time of under sixteen hours, in spite of a compass that had become faulty.

Byrd was sportingly received by his rivals back in Spitsbergen and ecstatically welcomed on his later return to America. The polar debate had finally been put to rest by this flight, or so everyone at the time believed. Yet soon, almost predictably, questions were being asked as to whether the plane in which Byrd and Bennett had flown could possibly have achieved the mileage it was supposed to have completed in the time they were airborne. Others who later flew the plane did not believe it could average the necessary speeds that had been described: academic calculations years later generally supported this analysis. Byrd had almost certainly come close, but yet again, it seemed it was impossible to be sure that he had actually made, or even seen, the Pole from his Fokker.

Byrd, meanwhile, unaware of the future questions that

would be raised in the light of his northerly achievement, was left to continue adding further distinctions to his *curriculum vitae*, in the south. These would include the permanent establishment of a US research base in Antarctica at 'Little America' in 1928, and the first flight over the South Pole a year later. Whether or not he had achieved the North Pole, he undoubtedly went on to prove that he was both a fine explorer and aviator.

Yet still, although nobody knew for certain, the race for the Pole possibly remained unfinished. If it did, it was a challenge that needed resolving. As it turned out, however, it would not be long after Byrd's flight before any remaining doubts were cast aside. For in the wake of Byrd's engine fumes, Amundsen, Ellsworth and Nobile finally ascended from Spitsbergen in their airship on 11 May 1926. A little over seventy hours later, they landed on the other side of the world in Alaska, having completed an undisputed passage over the North Pole in the interim. On reaching the top of the world on 12 May, they had even paused, hovering over the long-sought-after prize to drop the flags of their respective countries. The journey was not completely without incident. Ice tore holes in the balloon and increasingly built up on its shell, making navigation harder as the voyage continued, but nonetheless the adventurers completed their journey safely and, for once, uncontroversially.

The Pole, at last, had definitely been seen and definitely been conquered.

Chapter 8

'AN AWFUL PLACE':
Across Antarctica to the South Pole

James Cook was the first explorer to spark an
interest in Antarctica in the modern era. For
centuries there had been debate around whether a
southern continent existed, so the Captain, fearless
as ever, decided to try to find out once and for all
during his 1772–75 expedition.

C ook was a sceptic, believing that a large southern landmass probably did not exist. Once he had finished circumnavigating, becoming the first to enter the Antarctic Circle in the process, he saw no reason to change his mind. He had proven there was no *Terra Australis* at or above the level of the Antarctic Circle. If there did turn out to be anything further south then, as far as he was concerned, the world was welcome to it, for it would be a useless, ice-locked, barren wasteland.

For the next half century, that assessment was enough for most. By 1820, though, the world was becoming curious again: several countries wanted to know for sure what, if anything, lay at the bottom of the world. After decades of inactivity, Russia, America and Britain all now decided to lay claim to the discovery, after all, of some sort of Antarctic landmass. Fabian Gottlieb von Bellingshausen, a Russian, had certainly come close to it in January 1820 and indeed, had probably seen the continent, without realising at the time that it was something more than just an ice pack. The American sealer Nathaniel Palmer was in the region in the same year and also returned with a claim of having sighted Antarctica. So too did the British Captain Edward Bransfield, viewing Antarctica's northern tip at the Trinity Peninsula. He may also have become the first person to have set foot on the mainland. If he did not then John Davis, another American sealer, almost certainly did the following year.

In 1823, the Briton, James Weddell, sailed into the Antarctic sea that now bears his name, claiming to have set a new record for the furthest journey south of 74 degrees 34 minutes. He had surpassed Cook's previous best of 71 degrees 10 minutes by over 200 miles, although he had not sighted the Antarctic mainland even at that latitude. Some doubts continued to remain, then, about the existence of a southern continent.

Again there was a lull before anything further of real significance happened in the region. By 1840, though, a new race for knowledge between America, France and Britain was underway once more. The story of man on the Antarctic continent would at last begin in earnest. The quest for the South Pole, too, would only be a matter of time.

Charles Wilkes *(1798–1877)*

Charles Wilkes never strayed far from controversy during his career in the American navy. The expedition he led between 1838 and 1842, which is principally remembered for his discoveries in Antarctica, was a prime example of this. Indeed, such was the hullabaloo that followed in the mission's wake that its immediate successes were overshadowed by the fuss around Wilkes himself. This is a shame because the 'Wilkes Expedition', along with the two rival missions being undertaken separately by France and Britain at around the same time, truly began unveiling Antarctica for the first time.

The early career of Wilkes, at least, had been a little less fraught. Born in New York, he joined the US navy as a midshipman in 1818, after three previous years on merchant vessels. He progressed steadily, achieving the rank of lieutenant in 1826 and, a few years later, was made head of the Department of Instruments and Charts. It was in the wake of a Congressional bill approving the funding for an expedition to chart southern and Pacific waters, though, that Wilkes's big break came. It was not predestined as such. Four other men were first offered the command of the mission, from which they withdrew or declined, before it was proposed to Wilkes. Seeing the potential for fame and achievement it presented, however, Wilkes was happy to seize the opportunity.

So it was that with only limited experience of leading men at sea he set sail with a fleet of six vessels containing a total of more than 400 crew, artists and scientists in August 1838.

Although a key aim was to learn more about the Antarctic region, and in particular to help the commercial prospects of US whalers and sealers who were increasingly having to head further south in search of their catches, the Wilkes Expedition was about much more than just the southern seas. Consequently, it only actually entered the Antarctic for any kind of sustained period on two occasions in the course of its four-year duration. The rest of the time was spent surveying vast areas of other territory and collecting scientific specimens from as far afield as South America, the US west coast, Australia, New Zealand and, in particular, the Pacific Islands. On its return journey, the expedition would go on to complete a circumnavigation past the Philippines, through Asia, round the Cape of Good Hope and eventually, in June 1842, back to New York. In its wake, volumes of scientific and geographic papers and charts would be published and its collections would go a long way towards establishing the Smithsonian

Institution. Yet, in spite of this, the mission is still principally remembered for its few months spent in Antarctic waters.

The first foray to the deep south was undertaken between February and March 1839. It was largely unsuccessful. Four of the six vessels in the fleet, split into two groups of two, left from the Tierra del Fuego at the southern tip of America in an attempt to head as far south as possible. The *Peacock* and the *Flying Fish* set out on a southwesterly course; the *Porpoise* and the *Sea Gull* went due south. Of these, the *Flying Fish* eventually penetrated the furthest, having become separated from the *Peacock*, but it still did not manage to achieve as southerly a latitude as Cook, never mind James Weddell's record. More importantly, none of the fleet had found confirmatory evidence of the existence of an Antarctic continent. Defeated by the ice and bad weather, the ships limped back to South America within a couple of months, where the lack of progress would be compounded by the loss of the *Sea Gull* during their winter movements.

Unperturbed, though, Wilkes was back in the following Southern Hemisphere summer. This time he set out from Australia and would be far more successful. Four vessels again ventured south, Wilkes taking his flagship the *Vincennes* this time in place of the *Sea Gull*, and once more they began to become scattered. Nevertheless, Wilkes pressed on and in the middle of January reached a wall of ice. Two of the three ships caught up over the next few days, the *Flying Fish* eventually having to retreat to New Zealand, and together they moved westwards along the ice pack in the hope of finding an entrance to take them further south. It was here that they truly began to break new ground. On the date that Wilkes originally claimed to be 19 January 1840, but later tried to amend in typically controversial fashion to 16 January, they spotted 'Wilkes Land', confirmation of an Antarctic continent. A far-off mountain range was noted and mapped which, ironically, James Ross (*see* page 209), leading the rival British expedition slightly behind Wilkes, would later reveal as not existing at all, being merely a trick of refraction. Nevertheless, and in spite of damage to the *Peacock* which forced her to return to Australia, Wilkes continued along the ice barrier noting more land and ice shelves as he went. The *Porpoise* eventually retreated to New Zealand too, leaving the *Vincennes* alone to sight new land. By the time Wilkes was done, he had charted more than 1500 miles of Antarctica, albeit some of it erroneously, and was satisfied that he had become the first to confirm the existence of a continent-sized land mass at the bottom of the world.

In this there is some truth but, as ever with Wilkes, it is far from clear-cut. On exactly the same day that Wilkes originally claimed to have sighted the Antarctic continent, January 19 1840, Jules Sébastien César Dumont d'Urville's rival French expedition made an identical claim. This was why so much debate surrounded Wilkes's later attempt to move his first-sighting date to 16 January. Regardless, the French party certainly outdid Wilkes in one important respect. They actually made a landfall a couple of days after they had first spotted Antarctica, planting the French flag and claiming a stretch of the continent for France that D'Urville named in honour of his wife, Adélie Land. Even today, this area of Antarctica is still used by French scientists as a research base.

It was an unlikely success for d'Urville, by then a man nearing fifty years of age who suffered so badly from gout that he could barely walk. Before this expedition, he believed his career had already peaked with the discovery (and subsequent purchase for France) of the ancient and fabled statue the Venus de Milo, during an expedition to Greece. He had circumnavigated on an 1822–25 French scientific expedition, and between 1826 and 1829 confirmed the likely location of the demise of his famous exploring compatriot, Jean-François de Galaup, Comte de la Pérouse. On the same mission he had also discovered a number of Pacific islands and he undertook a fresh survey of the New Zealand coastline. Yet all of this would be surpassed in the grand expedition, similar to Wilkes's in both its global scope and its Antarctic ambition, which he was called to lead between 1837 and 1840. For all the mission's other work in the Pacific and elsewhere, and in spite of losing a significant number of men to scurvy and disease, d'Urville's voyage would be remembered principally for his flag-planting in Antarctica.

Wilkes had been aware of competitor activity before he even arrived back in the United States. Indeed, at the end of January 1840, D'Urville had encountered the *Porpoise* from Wilkes's expedition in the Antarctic itself. The two parties did not bother stopping to make contact. Wilkes also left a letter in Hobart for James Ross outlining his discovery of Wilkes Land, which the latter used as his basis for contesting some of the American's observations on his own expedition to the Antarctic. Thus, with disputes over who had seen the southern continent first and doubts raised over the accuracy of Wilkes's findings he was already surrounded by controversy when he arrived back in America.

To make matters far worse, though, he was rewarded for his four years of effort with a court-martial. Apparently, Wilkes was a hard task master – too hard for some – and he was convicted of illegally punishing certain members of his crew too harshly for pilfering the party's stores. Other charges were also brought against the American by his fellow officers but these, at least, did not stick.

Sadly, the controversy for Wilkes would not even end there. He did manage to salvage enough of his career to be entrusted with another vessel for use against the Confederacy on the outbreak of the American Civil War in 1861. Unfortunately, he saw fit to intercept a British mail ship, the *Trent*, in November 1861 and seize two Confederate commissioners to Britain, contrary to diplomatic protocol. At first this action was welcomed by his seniors, but when it became clear that the incident risked bringing Britain into the war on the side of the

Confederacy, President Lincoln distanced himself from the episode and released the prisoners. This and other subsequent squabbles resulted in Wilkes being retired and then court-martialled again in 1864, ending a career dogged by controversy for the previous twenty-five years.

Sir Ernest Henry Shackleton *(1874–1922)*

So Antarctica was definitely there. The next logical step for any explorer worth their salt, then, would be to investigate it more closely and eventually try to reach the South Pole. It would be an almost inevitable series of events. Yet after the initial rush by the US, France and Britain, virtually nothing of note happened again in the region for the next half century. For Ernest Shackleton, who was not even born until 1874, and in no position to begin making his name in the region until the turn of the century, this was no doubt regarded as a pleasing thing.

In the meantime, though, it was left to a small band of frustrated Antarctic enthusiasts to pick up the baton. The whalers and sealers, driven by business concerns, continued to do their utmost to promote interest in the waters around the southern continent. In 1894–95, the Norwegian Leonard Kristensen took one such commercial vessel to the region, making landings on several Antarctic islands and the mainland. One of the members of his team was Carsten Borchgrevink, who would later become significant for his own efforts to promote the Antarctic.

While Borchgrevink was trying to drum up interest back on the Australian lecture circuit (he was a Norwegian by birth but had migrated to Australia), it was left to Belgium, of all the maritime nations, to further the cause. In August 1897, a determined young lieutenant by the name of Adrien Victor Joseph de Gerlache de Gommery left Antwerp on a scientific expedition to the Antarctic. Among his crew members were Roald Amundsen (see page 291) and Dr Frederick A. Cook (*see* page 251). Unwittingly (or perhaps deliberately so, as some of his crew speculated at the time), de Gerlache's expedition became the first to overwinter in the Antarctic region after they were trapped in ice. Having arrived near Graham Land and sailed along a stretch of water that would later become known as Gerlache Strait, naming new islands as they went, they had headed farther south into the ice pack until they had become firmly wedged within it in March 1898. Almost a year would pass in cramped and difficult conditions before it eventually released them.

Meantime, Borchgrevink was back. Having failed to raise funds in Australia, he had turned to Britain. There he had eventually gained sponsorship from Sir George Newnes, a wealthy publisher, for a scientific and exploratory mission to Antarctica. As well as hoping to locate and ideally reach the South Magnetic Pole, Borchgrevink's intention was to be the first to overwinter on the continent itself. Setting out from the UK in August 1898, he landed on Antarctica in February 1899 and settled in for the southern winter at a place called Cape Adare. In spite of some hardships, mishaps and the sudden death of one of the crew members, the team came through the trial and were picked up in early 1900 for the journey home. In addition, they had worked out where the South Magnetic Pole lay and, although they had not been able to reach it, they had achieved a new furthest south record of 78 degrees 50 minutes.

What is more, Borchgrevink had succeeded in delaying the plans of Sir Clements Markham, the President of the British Royal Geographic Society (RGS), to send his own formal national expedition to the region. By diverting Newnes's money away from the RGS to himself, Borchgrevink had delayed the society from achieving the funds it needed to send out a rival undertaking. Not until the time of his return was it at last in a position to begin seriously considering an expedition and even then it would be another full year, the summer of 1901, before the *Discovery* mission, led by Robert Falcon Scott, actually set out. On board was Ernest Shackleton.

The man who Scott had appointed as a third lieutenant had needed to pull a lot of strings just to be included within the Antarctic party in the first place. Of Anglo-Irish descent, Shackleton had been born in Ireland but had moved to London in 1884 with his family. At sixteen he had joined the merchant navy and worked his way through the ranks over the next decade. By the turn of the century, he was Third Officer with the Union Castle Line merchant service, which was then engaged in ferrying troops to South Africa for the Boer War. On one such voyage, he met the son of Llewellyn Longstaff, who was the principal sponsor of Scott's proposed expedition. Shackleton persuaded his new acquaintance to give him an introduction to his father to present his case for being included in the National Antarctic Expedition.

Llewellyn Longstaff was impressed by Shackleton and recommended him to the RGS. Scott, only too aware of the importance of Longstaff's funding, was in little position to say no. Nonetheless, in later years he might wish that he had for Shackleton became one of his fiercest Antarctic rivals.

Initially, however, Scott and Shackleton worked together well. Indeed, Shackleton was one of only two men with Scott at the scene of the major achievement of the 1901–1904 expedition, a new furthest south record of 82 degrees 17 minutes (*see full details in Scott entry on page 282*). Unfortunately, though, Shackleton became ill during the trek with suspected scurvy and ended up having to be dragged back to base camp on a sledge. In spite of his protests, he was sent home on the grounds of his health on board a supply ship that came in the following summer. Shackleton probably felt a certain amount of resentment at this decision, which perhaps provided some of the motivation for what he would do next.

Having declined to take part in the Scott 'rescue' party in 1903, he almost immediately went on to propose his own follow-up Antarctic expedition to Sir Clements Markham, even while Scott was still away. Although initially refused, Shackleton could not let the idea drop and over the next few years began obtaining the sponsorship to put his dream in action. In February 1907 he formally announced his plan for a return mission to claim both the South Pole and the South Magnetic Pole, where the *Discovery* expedition had failed. Scott was most put out, not only because one of 'his' men was now squaring up in open competition without having consulted him first but, worse, Shackleton was also planning on using 'Scott's' Antarctic base in McMurdo Sound as his launch pad.

This would not do. In spite of the strain the chain of events put on the relationship between the two men, they later came to a public agreement. On Scott's insistence, Shackleton would not land in McMurdo Sound after all. Instead, he would concentrate his plans further along the coastline at either King Edward VII Land or Barrier Inlet. It would be a concession Shackleton would have cause to regret.

When Shackleton's '*Nimrod*' expedition finally got under way in August 1907, and subsequently arrived in Antarctica in early 1908, he found he physically could not land at either of his agreed destinations. Ice was barring his way and he soon realised that there was only one solution. He would have to retreat to McMurdo Sound and in doing so break his word to Scott, losing any remaining sense of honour among wider interested parties. When Scott later learnt of what had happened it certainly stretched their relationship to breaking point. Yet Shackleton's determination to reach the Pole was such that he was prepared to live with the consequences. In the event, he came very close to his goal.

Once the *Nimrod* team had seen off the 1908 Antarctic winter, the sledging parties split into two groups. Shackleton and three others would head for the South Pole. Another team, which included the Australian Douglas Mawson, would target the South Magnetic Pole.

Mawson, already a respected scientist, would go on to be an important explorer in his own right. Between 1911 and 1914, he would lead the Australasian Antarctic Expedition, aimed at mapping the thousands of miles of uncharted Antarctic territory that were closest to Australia. On one of the sledging forays undertaken during this mission, the two men with Mawson at the time died from accident and illness respectively, leaving the Australian on his own in the Antarctic wilderness.

Despite being himself sick and weak, he managed to claw his way back alone, to base camp and salvation. Between 1929 and 1931, with the Antarctic land-grab hotting up again, Mawson led two more expeditions to the region, which also helped cement Australia's claim to vast stretches of the continent's territory.

Similarly in 1908–1909, with Mawson as their youngest member, the South Magnetic Pole team did very well. In spite of ration shortages and injury, they reached their goal on 16 January 1909. By 5 February they had managed to rendezvous with the *Nimrod* and relay the details of their impressive achievement to excited crew members.

At this time, however, the Shackleton party were still out on the ice. They had not been quite as successful but, despite having to shoot most of their supply-dragging ponies, they had done well. On January 9 they had reached a new furthest south record of 88 degrees 23 minutes, smashing the previous best. Less than a hundred miles short of the Pole, however, a combination of dwindling food and poor weather had forced them to turn back. After a better return journey, they made contact with the *Nimrod* again in early March. All aboard safely, it steamed out of the region before the winter ice set in, to take home a party of heroes led by the soon-to-be-knighted Shackleton.

Yet in spite of his achievements Shackleton knew the South Pole race would be over before he could even have the opportunity to mount another expedition. Scott and Roald Amundsen (*see* page 291) would soon be engaged in rival missions for the prize Shackleton had so narrowly missed. Consequently, he was forced to turn his exploratory sights onto an even grander project: the crossing of mainland Antarctica from the Weddell Sea to the Ross Sea via the South Pole. It would be a mammoth undertaking of some 1800 miles, with no opportunity to return over the same ground and use known-supply depots, as had been the case on his first South Pole mission.

Such a task required two main teams. One would need to head to the Ross Sea and lay out advance supply depots to assist the cross-continental party on the second half of their overland journey. The other would need to enter the Weddell Sea, landing on that side of Antarctica and setting up a base before the overlanders among them began their marathon sledge journey.

The mission began on the eve of the First World War in 1914. Indeed, Shackleton even offered to postpone it in favour of turning the vessels and men to military service, but he was ordered to continue. As Shackleton made his way south towards the Weddell Sea aboard what would prove to be the aptly named *Endurance*, the Ross Sea support team steamed south from Australia on the *Aurora*. In case Shackleton arrived south in time to begin his journey during the 1914–15 Antarctic summer, the Ross Sea brigade were to begin laying out as many depots as they could as soon as they arrived on the continent in January 1915. If Shackleton did not appear that year, then they were to penetrate further inland the following season and create even more supply depots. They did exactly as instructed, ultimately losing three out of their ten men during their two years in the ice. Yet Shackleton never emerged from across the Antarctic mainland.

In fact, he never even made it to the mainland. Instead, he was engaged in one of the greatest adventure survival stories of all time. As she made her way into the Weddell Sea, the *Endurance* had become frozen into the ice, a pinching from which she would never escape afloat. For ten months she drifted with the Antarctic floe until in November 1915, the *Endurance* finally gave in to the relentless ice pressure and sank. Shackleton had time to remove the ship's boats and supplies on to a floe, but now they were stuck on a piece of ice hundreds of miles from the nearest signs of civilisation. Eventually in April, they drifted into open sea and, marginally more comforting, spotted land, albeit remote and barren, in the form of a place called Elephant Island. They managed to land on the island and from there Shackleton plotted their escape.

Their only hope of salvation was to reach the whaling outpost in South Georgia, some 800 miles away. Shackleton split his team into two, taking five men with him on one of the boats and leaving the majority of the men to await his rescue on the island. In just two weeks, in spite of freezing conditions, appalling weather and terrible seas, they were within sight of their destination. Unfortunately, landing the boat proved to be an equally difficult prospect and it took them two days to eventually evade rocks and rough seas and finally dock the boat.

Even now, they were not saved. In fact, they still literally had a mountain to climb. The party had landed on the opposite side of South Georgia from where the whaling station and salvation lay and the only way to reach it was across the island's unconquered mountain peaks. So with the same determination that Shackleton had shown in the last year, he and two of his men simply got on with it. For the next day and a half, with barely five minutes sleep in the middle, they traversed the rocks before, at last, they made contact with salvation!

Once the whaling station manager realised who the men were – he did not recognise them in their bedraggled state at first – and had come to terms with their remarkable story, the rescue operation began. The next day the three men on the other side of the island were picked up by ship. Afterwards, it was off to find the Elephant Island party, Shackleton of course amongst the rescuers. This proved to be no easy task as ice and other technical problems hampered the operation but eventually, after several attempts, they reached the stranded men at the end of August 1916. They had all survived.

Still, though, the expedition was not finished for Shackleton. He had to retrieve the survivors of the Ross Sea party. By December he was in New Zealand ready to head south aboard the *Aurora* which in the interim had also spent a period locked in the ice. It had eventually escaped and in January 1917 the boat reached the seven men stranded in Antarctica, before steaming back to New Zealand once more. At last the tortuous mission was over.

Ideas for Antarctic adventure were still not quite out of Shackleton's system, however. Although he had endured a remarkable survival story, his last mission had essentially been a failure. He longed for one more trip to the south to try to achieve something more of note and the opportunity came in 1921. By January 1922 he was in South Georgia again. The island of his earlier salvation, however, would now become the location of his final resting place. For no sooner had he arrived, than he suffered a massive heart attack and died.

It was the best part of four decades before anyone actually achieved Shackleton's earlier goal of crossing the Antarctic continent by land. The Englishman Sir Vivian Ernest Fuchs, supported at the Ross Sea end by a team headed by Sir Edmund Hillary, later to be one of the first men to scale Everest (*see* page 363), led a team across Antarctica between 1957 and 1958. Their route was virtually identical to the one that Shackleton had so wanted to attempt himself, but been denied the chance.

Robert Falcon Scott *(1868–1912)*

Back in February 1907, however, Robert Falcon Scott was rather unhappy. Not only had he failed to come close to the South Pole during his 1901–1904 expedition to Antarctica, but now one of his subordinates on that mission, Ernest Shackleton, was planning to usurp him. He would become even more upset when he later learned that Shackleton had gone back on his word not to use 'Scott's' base of McMurdo Sound as his launching point for the Pole.

Such was the perceived code of honour that surrounded exploration at that time. As the man who had led the first expedition, Scott believed, according to the protocol of the age, that it was his unspoken right to head another mission before any of his compatriots struck out on their own. Certainly it was his exclusive 'right' to use McMurdo Sound. Shackleton's personal ambition, however, smashed apart these cosy presumptions. And the Norwegian Roald Amundsen would shortly afterwards shatter any presuppositions Shackleton had left untouched, with his own South Pole attempt. To add insult to injury, in January 1907 Scott had outlined his own plans for a return expedition to Antarctica but could not obtain the funds to support it!

So it would be forgivable if Robert Scott were permitted a wry grin and a relieved sigh when he heard of Shackleton's failure, albeit a close run thing, to reach the South Pole. That left the way still open for Scott to have another go and, by the end of 1909, the money was at last starting to trickle in. Yet, as an honourable man he certainly would not, publicly at least, have admitted as much. Indeed, even after he had been affronted by the declaration of Shackleton's plans to launch his own expedition, he still insisted it was his duty to support it because, 'The first thing is to defeat the foreigners'.

Misplaced as some of this gentlemanly sentiment might seem now, and perhaps even at the time in the ruthless world of exploration, there is no doubting Scott's credentials as a leader. Indeed, it was probably this principled side which, as much as anything else, endeared him to the vast majority of his men. He had been well brought up and perfectly schooled for the Antarctic tasks that would ultimately prove his destiny. As early as 1887 Sir Clements Markham, President of the Royal Geographic Society, had earmarked Scott as a potential candidate to lead his countrymen on any mission to the southern continent. Twelve years later, the reality of such an expedition was much closer and it was on Markham's encouragement that Scott applied to be at its head. After much bickering between the Royal Society and the Royal Geographic Society over their preferred men and, equally, over the actual object of the undertaking, Scott was approved for its leadership. These beginnings would evolve into the 1901–1904 'Discovery' expedition.

By this point in his career, Scott was ready to assume such a responsibility. Born and brought up in Devon, England, he had first taken to the seas as a midshipman in his early teens. He worked hard and was a fast learner, progressing through the navy's ranks during tours of duty on several ships in his first years. A later spell at college in Greenwich completed his maritime studies, after which Scott continued working his way up the career ladder. In June 1900, news of his appointment to lead the Antarctic expedition came through and by the following summer he was ready to depart England for the next phase of his life's work.

Even as the King and Queen, on the Isle of Wight, waved off Scott and his crew aboard the *Discovery* there still remained some confusion about the exact purpose of the expedition. Was it primarily scientific, exploratory or an attempt on the Pole? In the end it would become all three. Scott's team would have plenty more time on their hands than they had originally anticipated as they were forced to stay locked in the Antarctic ice. Another dimension to the expedition would also evolve, although Scott would have no way of knowing this until he returned to the Antarctic some years later. Their two winters in the southern ice would be the perfect training ground for some of the now famous names who would accompany him on his 1910–11 'dash' for the Pole. Edward Wilson and Edgar 'Taff' Evans, as well as several others who would be part of that mission's support team, were with Scott in 1901. As, of course, was Ernest Shackleton.

So what did this initial Scott expedition achieve? Well, even before he had docked, ahead of his first winter at the bottom of the world in early 1902, Scott had discovered a new stretch of Antarctic territory which he named King Edward VII Land. They then successfully established winter quarters in McMurdo Sound, 'Scott's' base, and undertook preparatory sledging and scientific work over the next months. It was not all positive, though. During these early sledging missions one man, George Vince, fell over a cliff and was killed and several others suffered from frostbite.

Nevertheless, in November 1902 Scott and a number of his men set off on a sledging mission aimed at pushing as far south as possible, perhaps even to the Pole. The 'main' party, comprising Scott, Shackleton and Wilson, who had been supported for the earlier part of their journey by other crew members, eventually reached their new furthest south record of 82 degrees 17 minutes. At this point they were forced to turn back due to health and other problems. It was not the Pole but it was still a fine achievement for virgin Antarctic explorers.

The expedition ended controversially as it stayed another year in the region against orders. Not that there was much Scott could do: the *Discovery* remained trapped in her icy harbour through the Southern Hemisphere summer. They were not short of food or fuel – the arrival of a supply ship had seen to that – and Scott saw no need to abandon ship. The British government did not necessarily agree, though, pointedly sending two ships to collect the men in the following year with instructions to leave the *Discovery* behind if she did not break free. Fortunately, she did, although Scott still felt that he had been left with the slight taint of egg on his face which undermined his perceived abilities as a leader. He should not have worried, though. The extra year had enabled the team to augment their scientific achievements, collect more specimens and undertake additional exploratory sledging journeys. They were welcomed back by most as heroes, Scott was promoted and the mission was judged a success.

But he still had not made the Pole and neither had Shackleton between 1907 and 1909 so Scott wanted the opportunity for another crack. In spite of the initial difficulty in raising the money, the majority of the required funds were in place by early 1910 and Scott was able to purchase the *Terra Nova* as his expedition's ship. Come the middle of the year, Scott and his crew were on their way, along with the motor sledges and ponies that they hoped would help them achieve their goal. By early January 1911 they were back at McMurdo Sound, having established their winter quarters. Depot-laying sledge journeys were begun ahead of the all-out assault on the Pole that was planned for the following Antarctic summer. They had to achieve as much as possible before winter set in because by now they knew they were in an all-out race for the Pole. Roald Amundsen had sent word of his intentions to make a similar assault the following summer. Their worst fears were further confirmed when members of Scott's support team actually bumped into the Norwegians in the Bay of Whales making their own preparations. The rival sprinters were in their blocks.

Nonetheless, the desire for scientific gain from the expedition was not abandoned by Scott and the winter in particular provided the opportunity to make more progress. Yet the Pole was their main goal and the expedition began in earnest at the start of November when Scott and his support teams finally started their push towards it. By then, unknown to the Englishman, Amundsen was already on his way and making rapid progress. Scott, however, concerned for the survival of his ponies in the cold, had chosen to delay his start until November, even though he knew that this decision would probably lose him time to the Norwegians and their dog teams.

He might as well not have bothered. The ponies proved ineffective and either died as they walked along or later had to be shot; the motor-sledges proving similarly unreliable. For Scott and his team it was back to man-sledging, not an entirely forlorn mode of transport but slower than dog-sledging. Moreover, although Scott was not to know it, the futile delays at the beginning were probably what would cost him his life.

Before tragedy, however, there was first some kind of triumph. In spite of all the hardships they had endured, and their severely weakened condition, Scott and his final polar party of Wilson, Evans, Captain Oates and Henry Bowers became, on 18 January 1912, the first British team to reach the South Pole. But they were not the first ever to stand on the spot, for Amundsen and his men had beaten them to it by more than a month. In spite of some inevitable dejection on finding the remnants of the Norwegians' camp, they had still achieved their stated goal in a fashion which, unlike the murky outcome of the race for the North Pole, could not be disputed. Although, as it turned out, they had not been the first, they could still take plenty of pride in their achievement which would nonetheless ensure them some kind of immortality.

Sadly, though, the final fate of the expedition's members would probably contribute to this outcome as much as their success in reaching the Pole itself. For within a little over two months Scott and the other four of the polar team were dead. They had set out on the return journey from the Pole weak and low on supplies, but knowing at least that they had a number of depots strewn out along the way back, where they could pick up food and fuel. Although there were sometimes difficulties in finding the depots and Evans, in particular, was growing weaker by the day, the journey still progressed according to plan until mid-February. Then, however, Evans collapsed and died. To make matters worse, it was now late in the season and the weather was starting to turn. Frostbite was kicking in and there was a shortage of oil for warmth because much of the fuel stored at the depots had leaked away during the summer.

All of these factors contributed to their demise but it was the weather, above all else, that sealed their fate. Blizzards and a strong wind continued to hamper their progress. Oates, too weak to continue and certain that he was holding up the remaining team, fell on his sword by stepping out of the tent one morning with the now immortal words, 'I am just going outside and may be some time.' His body was never found.

Just eleven miles from their next depot, where a support team with dogs awaited them, the remnants of the mission were finally stopped in their tracks. Unceasing blizzards pinned them to their tent where, without food and fuel, and increasingly weak and affected by frostbite, their fate was sealed. Scott's last diary entry came on 29 March 1912.

It would not be until November that a search party finally found the tent. By then, all that was left to do was retrieve Scott's last letters and journal, from which the story of the expedition's demise was obtained, and then cover the bodies in snow, along with the tent in which they lay.

Scott had conquered the Pole but the elements, in turn, had conquered him.

Roald Amundsen *(1872–1928)*

As Robert Scott was slowly perishing in his final snow-choked camp, Roald Amundsen had, by that stage, already reached Tasmania and had broken the news of the Norwegian conquest of the South Pole to the world. It was a starkly contrasting picture, highlighting just how differently the fortunes of the two rival teams had panned out. Yet that was typically the way with Amundsen. Where others struggled and, as with the British expedition, so often lost their lives in the pursuit of polar goals that had been chased for centuries, the Scandinavian almost effortlessly ticked them off one by one. Indeed, where the South Pole prize would doubtless have been considered a lifetime's achievement for Scott or almost any other adventurer, it would turn out to be merely one of many subzero successes for Amundsen. Of all the polar explorers he was surely the greatest.

Although being the first to reach the South Pole would not be the Norwegian's only major feat, it was almost certainly his finest. Yet, ironically, it was the one prize that he never particularly wanted at all. The North Pole had always been Amundsen's goal and it remained so almost right up until the minute that he was aboard the *Fram* heading south. Indeed, he had been desperate to join Nansen (*see* page 234) aboard the same ship for his Arctic attempt in 1893, but circumstances did not conspire in Amundsen's favour. Nevertheless, he persisted and was preparing his own North Pole attempt when news of the apparent success of Peary (*see* page 243) came through in 1909. Beaten to his primary target (or so he thought at the time) the Norwegian simply switched to a secondary one. If he could not be the first to the North Pole, then he would be the first to the South instead.

Unlike Scott, Amundsen was unaffected by concerns about 'gentlemanly' conduct or the 'honourable' explorers' code. Whilst by no means of a disrespectful nature, the most important factor for Amundsen was, as far as possible, beating the competition to the 'big' achievements. With the North Pole 'gone', the South Pole was the next best thing. Scott and everyone else would just have to deal with that.

So determined was the Scandinavian that he should not be thwarted in his change of plan, that he did not even tell most of his crew, or any of his sponsors, of the new goal when the expedition left Norway aboard the *Fram* in August 1910. At that point everyone, including Scott, thought they were going to continue on their expedition to the Arctic. Allegedly, the principal aims of the mission were scientific, not competitive, so logic dictated that it should not have been affected at all by the fact that the North Pole race had been won. One of the few who did not agree was Amundsen. But determined as he was, the Norwegian was canny enough to realise that if he announced his change of plan too early, he might be prevented from going at all.

So he told almost no-one until the *Fram* stopped at Madeira in early September 1910. At this point, he broke the news to his stunned crew who agreed to accompany him anyway. Revealing the change was left to Amundsen's brother on the island. Even then, however, he did not begin sending telegraphs announcing the new plan until October, one of which Scott was destined to pick up on his way south, by which stage Amundsen was irretrievably on his way. It was this year-long 'deception', perhaps even more so than Shackleton's earlier affront, that upset Scott and his 'honourable' supporters. Yet for Amundsen, that was a minor concern: the only important thing was to win the race for the South Pole.

And win it he did with almost effortless ease. Although he had started out from Europe some two months after Scott, he still beat him to the mark by over a month, arriving at the South Pole on 14 December 1911. The difference of several weeks not only enabled Amundsen to claim the polar prize but also escape with his life by avoiding the inclement March weather that claimed Scott. As with the amalgamation of factors that contributed to the Englishman's demise, there were a number of reasons for Amundsen's success, despite the late change to his plans.

For one, he had been to the Antarctic before. He had served on de Gerlache's 1897–99 expedition to the region, even taking control of the *Belgica* for a period when the leader fell ill. Having overwintered in the Antarctic already, therefore, Amundsen was well aware of what to expect. Secondly, he had chosen to dock at the Bay of Whales. This location gave him a sixty-mile head start on Scott. The fact that Scott's life would ultimately be lost by a margin of eleven miles serves to underline how crucial this difference could be. The Norwegians set off earlier in the southern summer season than Scott, which meant that they missed the worst of the weather that Scott later encountered. Perhaps, most crucially, they had been able to do this because they were using dogs to haul their sledges, animals that were able to withstand cooler temperatures and move faster over the snow than Scott's ponies. Furthermore, Amundsen's team travelled light and were all accomplished skiers.

Not that Amundsen's success was entirely without problems. He initially set off in September, too early in the season, and was forced to return within a few days. The aftermath of the incident caused friction, to the point that he was forced to divide his party and only take the reduced number of four to the Pole: Oscar Wisting, Helmer Hanssen, Sverre Hassel and Olav Bjaaland. En route they had to conquer the formidable Axel Heiberg Glacier, as well as other dangerous terrain, and they frequently encountered hostile weather. Yet compared to the labours of the Scott party their journey to and from the bottom of the world was impressively trauma-free. Just over a month after they had reached the Pole they were back at the *Fram* and soon charging towards Tasmania.

It would be typical to add that at this stage Amundsen became world famous for his success, yet he was already internationally renowned. If Amundsen had achieved one target, in the form of the South Pole, that explorers had only been seriously chasing for a few decades, he had already accomplished another they had been pursuing for centuries. Between 1903 and 1906 he had led a team that at last became the first to conquer the Northwest Passage that had so frustrated Frobisher, Parry, the Rosses and Franklin alike (*see* Chapter 6). Indeed, Franklin had been one of Amundsen's boyhood heroes. Yet unlike the forlorn British explorer, the Norwegian did not perish in the Passage but conquered it with relative ease.

Much of the time Amundsen passed in the ice after beginning his journey through Baffin Bay and on to Lancaster Sound was spent near the location of the demise of Franklin's party on King William Island. For Amundsen, though, this was not a scene of despair but of efficient scientific work. Once again, he had been forced to disguise his exploratory ambitions under the veil of science in order to obtain sponsorship and so spent the best part of two years in the channel making magnetic observations. He confirmed that the North Magnetic Pole did in fact move over time, ensuring that his expedition would be hailed as a success anyway, before steaming on through the icy waters to complete the rest of the Passage. On his exit from the northern channel, his vessel became iced in for another winter, so rather than wait for the season to pass before breaking the news, Amundsen simply sledged the 500 miles to the nearest telegraph point in Alaska to pass on word of his feat!

Nevertheless, with the South Pole and the Northwest Passage safely tucked under his belt, Amundsen still could not relinquish the dream of his primary passion:

the North Pole. Even if he might not be the first, he was still determined to make it there. Consequently, once the First World War had passed he led a new expedition to try to drift to the North Pole on the ice, 'Nansen-style', aboard his own purpose-designed ship, the *Maud*. On this occasion his primary goal remained stubbornly out of reach but, nevertheless, Amundsen completed the traversing of the Northeast Passage around Russia between 1918 and 1920, another tick on every polar adventurer's checklist.

Still desperate to reach the North Pole and, in spite of everything he had achieved, probably at the time of his lowest ebb, Amundsen later found the partner who would help him realise his goal. Lincoln Ellsworth funded an aeroplane attempt on the Pole in 1925, on which he flew with Amundsen. This failed, but the next year the two men returned and succeeded in an airship piloted by the Italian Umberto Nobile. Although Amundsen did not realise it at the time, his expedition had become the first to definitely reach the North Pole (*see* Chapter 7). In the process of their journey they had also gone on to cross the entire Arctic ice pack from Europe to Alaska.

Ironically, having conquered the Northwest Passage,

the Northeast Passage, the North Pole and the South Pole without harm, Amundsen would lose his life in the ice on a mission that had no exploratory goals at all. Umberto Nobile had gone back to the Arctic in his airship in 1928 and had crashed. Even though Nobile had been the member of the 1926 Amundsen-Ellsworth North Pole team who had caused the most friction and with whom Amundsen had personally fallen out, the Norwegian selflessly insisted on being in the rescue party that tried to go to his aid. The plane that Amundsen boarded for the effort in June 1928 was lost a few hours into its search, along with one of the greatest explorers of all time. With further irony, Nobile turned up at the end of the month anyway, rescued by a Russian ship.

The search now began in vain for Amundsen. Among the would-be rescuers was an American by the name of Louise Arner Boyd. She flew in a mission she had funded, covering thousands of miles of Arctic territory in the forlorn hope of finding the Norwegian. In time, Boyd herself would go on to become a noted Arctic adventurer. She undertook scientific expeditions to Greenland in the 1930s, and later to the Arctic Sea off Norway. She carried out polar magnetic studies during the Second

World War for the US government and, in 1955, became the first woman to fly over the North Pole. At the time, she was 68 years old.

Amundsen, who was himself in his mid-fifties when he perished, would have understood the desire that compelled Boyd to keep on heading into the polar regions even into old age, for the Norwegian was more driven than most. Indeed, it was this very drive that had pushed him into achieving so much: above all, the first conquest of the South Pole.

Chapter 9

A FURTHER SHORE:

Crossing Australasia

The unveiling of Oceania, particularly Australia and New Zealand, is commonly associated with the grand voyages of Captain Cook (*see* page 351) in the 1760s and 1770s. In fact, Dutch traders and explorers had visited many areas in Australasia a hundred and fifty years earlier, before they began to lose interest in the region later in the seventeenth century.

Even so, there were others who sailed into Australasian waters long before Cook came along. One example is William Cecil Dampier, an Englishman. He spent much of his early seafaring career as a pirate. The years 1686–91 saw him spend a large amount of time in both Asia and the Pacific, eventually journeying down to the huge land mass that would eventually become known as Australia. The English navy was so interested in his experiences in the region that it later forgave him his buccaneering ways and asked him to head an official expedition there. Between 1698 and 1699 he undertook this mission in a shoddy vessel barely suited to such a long voyage. Nonetheless he managed to explore a stretch of western Australian coastline as well as discover 'New Britain' near New Guinea before his ship later gave out on him and he was wrecked off Ascension Island.

Even by the 1760s, Cook was not alone in Oceania. Indeed, the French, in the form of the circumnavigator Louis Antonie de Bougainville were also there before the English captain. Between 1766 and 1769 he visited many islands in the South Pacific and later encountered the Great Barrier Reef off Australia's east coast. The potential that this great geographical feature offered for shipwrecking, though, persuaded the Frenchman to sail away again before he reached Australia itself.

Nevertheless, it was Cook's travels and the subsequent British establishment of a colony in New South Wales that prompted another flurry of exploratory activity in the region, picking up where the Dutch had left off more than a century before. Initially most investigations remained water-based but, soon, the sheer scale of land to be opened up within Australia in particular was too tempting for explorers keen to make a name for themselves to ignore.

The race was on to reveal the continent. As ever, lives would be lost and heroes made before the region's secrets finally submitted themselves to the world.

Abel Janszoon Tasman *(c.1603–c.1659)*

The first European to land in Australia, and in so doing bring a consciousness of its existence to the wider world, was Willem Janszoon. In 1606, while trading and exploring in the Asian islands, the Dutchman reached the northern tip of the continent in the area of the Gulf of Carpentaria. Over the ensuing decades other Dutch merchants periodically touched on parts of Australia's northern, western and possibly southern coastlines but much of this new land was left unexplored. It was not until 1642 that one of the early, great Australasian explorers, Abel Tasman, arrived in the region. Ironically, he did not land on the Australian mainland at all during his most famous first voyage of discovery, but he did prove the limit of the new land's southern extent and made several important discoveries in the surrounding seas.

Like so many of his compatriots who had been in the vicinity over the previous decades, Tasman's principal role was commercial. He worked for the powerful Dutch East Indies Company, who had established a significant base at Batavia (modern day Jakarta) in Indonesia. Its visionary Governor-General, Antony Van Diemen, was keen to expand the company's commercial influence in the region by seeking out and discovering new lands and markets. Tasman was a key part of the Governor's plan to achieve this goal.

Prior to his famous 1642 expedition, Van Diemen had already sent Tasman on one mission into the unknown. The explorer had captained one of two ships sent towards the Japan area in June 1639, under the overall command of a man named Matthijs Quast. Their goal was new sources of gold and silver rumoured to be easily available on certain supposed islands thought to be located to the east of Japan. Despite extensive investigations covering a significant area in their target region, they would be disappointed, although they did improve Dutch knowledge and the mapping of certain Philippine islands en route.

Van Diemen's interest now turned southward. This time Tasman would be engaged at the head of the expedition that would make the Dutchman's name renowned. Van Diemen was keen to know if an undiscovered great southern continent, which had long been rumoured and could perhaps become a base for a new trading route via South America and back to Europe, lay at lowly latitudes rarely touched on by sailors. Alternatively, the suspected continent of Nova Hollandia (New Holland, later renamed Australia), as encountered by earlier Dutch traders, might stretch continuously southwards or, if it did not, provide a new passage round its southern coastline to Chile. Consequently, Tasman was instructed to sail at a latitude below 50 degrees south and either find the southern continent or disprove its existence and then, ideally, continue on to Latin America.

Tasman left Batavia in August 1642 with two ships, the *Zeehaen* and the *Heemskerck*, en route for his first stop in Mauritius. From there he was to travel south to his prescribed line of latitude and then sail eastwards. After over a month in Mauritius conducting repairs and re-supplying, Tasman headed south in October, as instructed. He soon found, however, that it was extremely difficult to navigate in the lowly latitudes that he had been assigned, so he sailed eastward along a line nearer to 40 degrees instead. It was this decision, in November 1642, that resulted in what perhaps was his most famous discovery. He encountered a landfall that he named Van Diemen's Land, in honour of his Governor, off what is now known to be the southern tip of Australia. In time, the island (although Tasman did not know it was such) would be renamed Tasmania instead, after its discoverer. Initially struggling to find a sound landing spot, Tasman eventually docked in Tasmania in early December and claimed it on behalf of the Dutch.

The explorer now continued eastwards on the same latitude and on 13 December 1642 discovered New

Zealand. Although it was another significant finding for Tasman, it would not necessarily be a happy one. Having made his way up South Island and beyond Cape Farewell into Cook Strait, which separates the two main islands of New Zealand, he finally anchored in its more sheltered waters. Some of his men were soon involved in a hostile encounter with native Maoris, however, which left three of them dead. Grimly, Tasman named the spot 'Murderer's Bay'. Furthermore, he went on to mistake Cook Strait for a bay, therefore concluding that it did not provide a short cut between the two islands into the Pacific and on to South America. He turned around and promptly left the scene of his misfortune, heading north and, once clear of New Zealand, northeast.

In January 1643, Tasman landed on a number of the Tongan islands. From there he decided to head northwest and, soon after, discovered the Fijian islands. Slightly confused about his exact position, the explorer continued to head northwest in the hope of encountering more familiar waters. Eventually, he reached the known north coast of New Guinea and from there made his way back to Batavia, arriving in June 1643.

Harshly, the voyage was not considered particularly

successful by the Dutch East Indies Company. Tasman
had completed a ground-breaking journey of unrivalled
discovery in Oceania, had proved there was a sea passage
beneath Nova Hollandia and had outlined the beginnings
of a route to South America via this course. Yet, crucially,
he had not made the sea crossing through to Chile to
prove this passage and, in all his other landings, he had
found little evidence of precious metals or highlighted
the possibility of useful trading partnerships with some
of the new islands. The Dutch East Indies Company was
a business after all and while discovery was all very well,
it was not an end for its own sake.

Nevertheless, Tasman remained in high enough
regard to be sent on another exploratory mission in 1644.
This would bring him into contact with the Australian
mainland but the outcome of the voyage would not be
as ground-breaking as his 1642–43 foray. Departing from
Batavia in February 1644 he did, however, confirm that
the land mass of 'Nova Hollandia' continued all the way
from Cape York, Australia's northern tip, to a sizeable
portion of western Australia's coastline. Prior to this he
had sailed close to the shores of southern New Guinea
before, significantly, mistaking the Torres Strait, in the

stretch of water between this land and Australia, for a bay. He did not, therefore, unveil the eastern side of Australia but instead turned south and then west to map the Gulf of Carpentaria. From here he continued his journey westwards along the 'Nova Hollandia' coastline before returning to Batavia.

Again, Tasman's findings were not largely welcomed as his three vessels, the *Zeemeuw*, the *Bracq* and the *Limmen*, had failed to satisfy the eastward trading route goals of his company or discover new gold and silver. Dutch interest began to wane in Australasia and its lands would ultimately be left for other European powers to claim.

For all the Dutch East Indies Company's lack of interest in these geographical discoveries, though, Oceania was at last beginning to take its place on the global map. And for much of that, the world would have Abel Tasman to thank.

Matthew Flinders *(1774–1814)*

With the exception of occasional forays such as those of William Dampier, little more exploration was actively undertaken to reveal the remaining mysteries of Australasia for over a century. Not until the arrival of people like de Bougainville and Cook in the 1760s and 1770s did many of the region's remaining gaps begin to be filled in. Nevertheless, even towards the turn of the nineteenth century there was still uncertainty about certain parts of the Australian coastline, with much of it remaining unexplored in any great detail. Step forth Matthew Flinders, first circumnavigator of the continent of Australia.

It is true that Tasman had indirectly rounded the Australian continent in a wide sweep during his 1642–43 expedition from Indonesia to Mauritius to Tasmania to New Zealand to Tonga to Fiji and back to Indonesia again. He had, however, been out of sight of the Australian mainland for the entire journey – indeed, he probably did not even realise the extent of what he was bypassing – such that it was left to the eighteenth century explorers to begin to fully appreciate the sheer magnitude of the continent. Flinders, therefore, was the first to circumnavigate Australia itself with that end as his specific goal, mapping the coastline and unveiling unexplored stretches as he went.

The scene of Flinders' eventual fame could hardly

have been further from his starting point in life. He was born half the world away near Boston, Lincolnshire in England, the son of a physician. It was expected that Matthew would follow the family line into a medical career but from his early teenage years, inspired by the story of *Robinson Crusoe*, his heart was set on adventure. So, in 1789, he joined his first ship in Kent and began learning the ropes. Within two years he was working for the notorious Captain William Bligh on a successful and mammoth voyage to Tahiti, collecting breadfruit to be transported and sold to the West Indies. Bligh had attempted a similar undertaking from 1787 to 1789 when his crew on the *Bounty* had mutinied and set him adrift in a small lifeboat in the Pacific Ocean. Amazingly, the captain had managed to navigate his vessel over 3,000 miles on open seas to eventual salvation. On returning to England in 1790, he desired little more than to be able to undertake his original mission again. Within a year he was granted his wish. Flinders made a good impression on Bligh and it was here that his navigational skills and map-making abilities were initially recognised. It was also a journey that would bring him in touch with a portion of the Australian coastline for the first time.

On his return in 1793 Flinders would be engaged in action against the French for a period, again distinguishing himself. In spite of the excitement of war, though, the Englishman was set on adventure further afield and, in 1795, he returned to Australia aboard the *Reliance*. While sailing south, Flinders was reacquainted with a Lincolnshire doctor he had met during his youth, George Bass. Together the two men would go on to make several important discoveries. Their alliance would also act as the perfect training partnership for even more significant voyages later headed by Flinders alone.

On arrival in Australia, Bass and Flinders, along with Bass's servant William Martin, set out to explore the coastline immediately to the south of Sydney. Bass had brought with him a tiny boat, the *Tom Thumb*, for the task. It was barely suitable for the waters they encountered but, nevertheless, their initial explorations were productive and land for future settlement was noted. A second voyage discovered Port Hacking. Realising that their vessel was not equal to their ambition, however, they acquired a larger whaleboat. In 1797, they took it round Cape Howe, Australia's southeastern tip, and journeyed near to what is now the location of Melbourne. Over

300 miles of previously uncharted shoreline was mapped. From tidal observations, Bass also began to suspect that Tasmania (then still called Van Diemen's Land) was in fact an island and was not connected to the Australian mainland as had been previously assumed.

This suspicion resulted in Bass and Flinders' most significant expedition to date, between 1798 and 1799. They set out to prove that there was a channel between Tasmania and the Australian continent and they were successful. The strait between the two land masses now bears Bass's name. Their boat, the *Norfolk*, went on to circumnavigate and map Tasmania. The results of their work directly resulted in the founding of a colony there in 1803, at what is now the island's capital of Hobart.

In 1800, after also having taken the *Norfolk* up the Queensland coast in search of navigable inland rivers, Flinders sailed back to Britain. This return marked the end of his productive partnership with Bass. Indeed, within three years, Bass had disappeared off the face of the earth altogether after having been engaged in transporting a mercantile cargo across the Pacific. Perhaps his ship was wrecked or perhaps it was captured, with Bass being kidnapped by the Spanish, but either way he was simply never seen again. While Bass was fighting for his life, though, Flinders was back in Australia, completing his most important exploratory mission.

On arriving back in Britain, Flinders had outlined a plan involving his return to the continent to Sir Joseph Banks, the famous botanist, explorer and influential president of the Royal Society. Flinders proposed completing the first circumnavigation of Australia, with the particular aim of providing a detailed and reliable map of its coastline. Banks supported the idea and used his influence to secure Flinders the command of the *Investigator* in 1801. Flinders grasped the opportunity to lead his own significant expedition, even though he was engaged and married shortly afterwards and would have to leave his new wife behind in England. His ship departed in July 1801 with the future legendary Arctic explorer John Franklin (*see* page 200) among the crew.

By the end of the year Flinders was off the southwestern tip of Australia at Cape Leeuwin and his survey began with the charting of Australia's southern coast. Among his early discoveries were the Gulf of St. Vincent near Adelaide and Kangaroo Island. He also found a French expedition at 'Encounter Bay', led by Nicolas Baudin, that was attempting to complete a similar task to Flinders himself. By May, the *Investigator* had reached Sydney where it was necessary to carry out repairs on the ship before continuing northwards. Efforts to maintain the vessel were largely in vain, however. Although she could still float, the *Investigator* was in such bad shape that Flinders was forced to give up his detailed survey after charting the Gulf of Carpentaria in northern Australia and, instead, simply concentrate on completing the continent's circumnavigation as quickly as possible. This, at least, he accomplished and by June 1803, he was back in Sydney. Although he had not been able to chart the entire continent to the level of detail he would have liked, he had nevertheless filled in most of the remaining gaps and completed high quality maps of a huge portion of the Australian coastline.

From his greatest triumph, though, Flinders was shortly afterwards at his nadir. After one abortive attempt to sail home from Sydney, he charted a small, poor-quality vessel called the *Cumberland* for the journey back to England in 1803. There were so many problems with the schooner that Flinders was forced to dock at the French island of Mauritius on his way home. Unfortunately, war had broken out in the meantime between England and France. Flinders was subsequently imprisoned there on spy charges for nearly seven years. Although he eventually obtained his freedom, Flinders' privations had taken their toll and his health never fully recovered. Within a few years he was dead.

Flinders' legacy would be his excellent maps of much of Australia's coastline, which were not bettered for many decades after his demise. In addition, he left behind a record of the first circumnavigation of Australia, *A Voyage to Terra Australis*. Above all, perhaps, it was Flinders' use of the word 'Australia' within this work when describing the entire continent, and his previous promotion of the term, that subsequently saw the adoption of the word as it is used today. Matthew Flinders had rounded Australia, mapped her and named her.

Robert O'Hara Burke *(1820–1861)* and William John Wills *(1834–1861)*

With the coastline of Australia fully mapped, the next goal for explorers of the great continent would be to begin understanding something of the geography of its interior. To this point, towns and villages had largely been restricted to the coast or nearby inland communities, yet beyond the settlements there was a vast landmass to investigate and chart. The lure was irresistible for certain entrepreneurs and adventurers alike and soon the quest for knowledge was under way.

One of the early goals was to understand what lay beyond the great Blue Mountain range, which separated the east coast of Australia from its interior. After several others had failed, Gregory Blaxland, William Lawson and William Wentworth finally pioneered a path across these mountains in 1813. A new portion of Australia's interior was consequently opened up for cattle grazing and settlement.

Others now pushed on even further. Captain Charles Sturt led several expeditions in the 1820s and 1830 in the vain hope of finding an inland sea. He discovered the Darling and Murray rivers and crossed the interior from Sydney to near the later site of Adelaide. Hamilton Hume, who explored the Darling River with Sturt in 1828, had earlier forged a similar inland path with William Hovell, between 1824 and 1825, to what would be the location of Melbourne. While Hume soon retired from exploring, though, Sturt continued investigating. In

1844, he set off northwards from Adelaide and came to within a couple of hundred miles of the centre of the continent.

Other areas of Australia were also tempting explorers. Edward John Eyre became the first adventurer to cross Western Australia between 1840 and 1841. He endured incredible hardships, water shortages and the murder of one of his team during the immense crossing from Adelaide to Albany. Earlier he too had unsuccessfully tried to reach the centre of Australia. Meanwhile, a Prussian, Friedrich Wilhelm Ludwig Leichhardt, was exploring Queensland and the Northern Territory. In 1844–45 he travelled overland from near Brisbane to Port Essington, close to Darwin. He later led two unsuccessful attempts to cross Australia from the Brisbane area to Perth from 1846–47 and again in 1848. On the last occasion his party vanished altogether, a mysterious disappearance that has never been solved.

Indeed, the ultimate goal for any overland Australian explorer had to be the crossing of the entire interior. Unlike Leichhardt, however, most sought to traverse it from the settlements in the south to the northern coastline. As well as the exploratory kudos associated with achieving such a goal, and the commercial opportunities it would open up for land speculators, a very practical reason for undertaking an expedition of this kind also emerged. By the late 1850s, Australia was in need of a telegraph link with the outside world. An overland route from the north coast to where the line would be laid from India to the colonies in the south would need to be found. Indeed, there were so many benefits in being the southern hub for such a link that the colonial governments actively competed against each other to obtain that status. One means by which they aimed to do this was to encourage explorers to complete the cross-continental trek through the incentive of a financial prize. In 1859, for example, the South Australia government offered £2,000 for the first to achieve this target. Not to be outdone, the Victorian parliament opted to lavishly equip its own expedition, at even greater expense. The man who would be appointed at its head was Robert O'Hara Burke.

The Irishman, who had first moved to Australia in 1853, was not necessarily an obvious choice for the mission's control. He had no bush experience, was not known for being any great leader of men, and had hitherto had a relatively undistinguished career. He had been something of a drifter, beginning his career in the Austrian cavalry, of all places, then returning to Ireland to join the police force. On arriving in Tasmania, then Melbourne, he continued pursuing police work until the Crimean War broke out in Europe. At this point Burke left Australia, planning to join the British army. Having failed in this quest, he returned to Victoria, continuing with police inspection work until the idea of the overland expedition emerged. He grabbed the opportunity presented to him. It was an unlikely choice of appointment that arguably played a large part in Burke losing his own life and that of some of his men.

Nevertheless, Burke was determined to succeed in being the first to cross the Australian interior, for the glory of himself and the people of Victoria. In particular he wanted to beat off the challenge of the rival South Australian bid, currently being pursued by John McDouall Stuart. The urgency this generated would also contribute to Burke's demise as he unwisely rushed to complete his mission through the intense heat of the Australian summer. It also resulted in his expedition being divided as their trek wore on, in order that an advanced party with insufficient supplies could press ahead in anticipation of being caught up by the food-bearers later. They were not.

When the Burke party set out from Melbourne on 21 August 1860, however, it was an optimistic expedition. They could not have hoped to be better equipped. They had food for two years, more than enough camels and horses to carry them and a fifteen-strong team. By the time they reached their first major checkpoint at Menindee in New South Wales in October, though, the team was already in disarray. Among other squabbles, Burke had fallen out with his second-in-command George Landells who subsequently left the expedition. In his place, the mission's surveyor William John Wills was promoted to be Burke's right-hand man.

Wills was also a relatively recent Australian immigrant, having arrived from England in 1853. He had subsequently acquired knowledge of astronomy, meteorology and surveying, working for the Melbourne Observatory from 1858. It was for these skills that Wills was initially employed by the expedition, but nevertheless he diligently stepped into the deputy's role.

Impatient with the progress of the mission, Burke, Wills and six other men now broke themselves off into an advanced party. They would make a dash for Cooper Creek, roughly at the halfway point of their continental crossing and send for the remainder of the supplies at a later date. It would prove to be another fatal decision.

The eight men reached Cooper Creek in November. The guide they had employed to take them to this point, William Wright, was now sent back to Menindee to bring forth the remainder of the expedition. He would, however, become delayed back at the base camp and did not set out from Menindee again until late January 1861. By then, Burke had already made another ominous decision. Bored of waiting, and worried about losing the race to Stuart, he had split his party again in December. Burke, Wills, John King and Charles Gray would press on as quickly as possible to the northern coast. The remainder, under William Brahe, would wait at Cooper Creek for their return as well as the arrival of the supply team.

Amazingly, the four men reached the Gulf of Carpentaria, their goal, in early February. They had done it! The first people to cross Australia's interior. They could not descend into the sea itself, due to impassable swamps near the northern coast, but they had reached the Flinders River delta and come within sight of the sea's tidal influence. But at what cost had they achieved their goal? The men were already weak from limited rations: they had clearly not brought enough supplies with them to complete the round trip without facing near starvation. The weather had turned. Heavy rains brought them fresh water but also crucially slowed progress. As they grew weaker on their return journey, resorting to having to eat their camels and horses, they became more cumbersome, further contributing to delays that would prove fatal.

Gray died of dysentery on April 17. After pausing to bury his body and then rest, another crucial time loss, the three remaining starving men limped back to Cooper Creek a few days later. Giving them up for dead, and determined to find out what had happened to the anticipated supplies from the Wright party, Brahe had left literally just a few hours previously. He had buried some supplies and left a letter in case Burke returned, but it would not be enough to sustain the party for long.

Rather than try to catch up with Brahe, Burke decided to try to reach a police outpost some 150 miles away at the aptly named Mount Hopeless. It was another forlorn decision. In their weakened state, the men struggled to even navigate in the right direction, let alone reach their target. After weeks of wandering around lost, only managing to sustain their survival because some friendly aborigines fed them for a period, they had to retreat, even more weakened, to Cooper Creek. Worse still, in the interim Brahe had met with Wright on his journey northward and returned to Cooper Creek with supplies just in case Burke had finally made it back. Yet because Burke had left no obvious signs that he had been there before lumbering off into the desert again, Brahe concluded that the men had still not returned while he had been away. They had missed each other again and, crucially, Brahe did not leave any more supplies at Cooper Creek, because he figured Burke and Wills were dead.

Within a few weeks they would be. Wills died first, then Burke in June 1861. Only King survived and, encountering some friendly aborigines again who fed him, managed to sustain himself until another rescue party finally found him in September. The bodies of Burke and Wills were taken back to Melbourne along with the news of their achievement. But nobody was celebrating.

John McDouall Stuart *(1815–1866)*

A colleague of John McDouall Stuart once described him as 'the king of the Australian explorers'. Yet, in many ways, he is also the forgotten explorer. Even in his own day, he returned home to Britain in relative poverty after many exploratory successes in Australia, where he passed away almost unnoticed. His quiet funeral, attended by only a handful of people, was in stark contrast to the crowds of mourners who lined the streets of Melbourne for Burke and Wills. Indeed, it is probably because of the furore surrounding the demise of Burke and Wills, and the fact that these two men managed to cross the continent first, that Stuart's achievements have perhaps been overlooked. They should not have been. He headed multiple expeditions which unveiled large parts of inland Australia and he was the first to lead a party across the continent and actually return again, his whole team alive. Indeed, in his leadership of five major expeditions, John McDouall Stuart never once lost a man.

The last three of Stuart's expeditions were explicit attempts to cross the Australian continent from south to north. Before this, though, he endured two decades of the toughest training conditions that would serve him well in his later forays. On arriving in Australia in 1839 from Scotland, the country of his birth, he began work as a surveyor in the land around Adelaide. This job brought him into contact with Charles Sturt who was also involved in similar work in the region at that time. It was an association that would lead to Stuart's later appointment on Sturt's 1844–45 push for the centre of Australia. Stuart would become second-in-command before the mission had finished, following the death of the original deputy James Poole. Although the team had to retreat just a few hundred miles short of their target, they had seen much previously uncharted territory and the experience would serve Stuart well in future.

On his return from the expedition, Stuart would continue building on his outdoor experience as a private surveyor of land in South Australia. It was not until 1858 that he would undertake his next major exploratory mission. It lasted for four months and it saw Stuart traipsing through South Australia and suffering great hardship but successfully finding swathes of potential new grazing land. A more ambitious expedition in the first half of 1859 would result in Stuart's team heading further northwards, almost to the edge of South

Australian territory, as the Scot sought to probe ever deeper inland.

By the end of the year, the interest of the colonies had very much turned to the complete crossing of the continent from south to north. Stuart was more interested than most. Before Burke and Wills had even begun mounting their own challenge, Stuart had already obtained the blessing of the South Australian government and was on his way in November 1859. Initially starting out with six other people in his team, Stuart had to let most of the men return home after rations started to run short. One man, William Kekwick, remained. After supplies had been replenished a new member, Benjamin Head, also joined the party at Chambers Creek. The three men set off northwards again and, in spite of the usual difficult conditions and ration hardships, were soon breaking new ground. Towards the end of April 1860, Stuart at last reached the long-sought-after goal of the centre of Australia. He named a nearby mountain after Charles Sturt, which was later renamed in honour of its discoverer, Central Mount Stuart.

Having passed the halfway point, the three men continued on in pursuit of their ultimate goal. More 'new' land was conquered as they headed northwards beyond Tennant Creek, until they were finally forced to turn back by hostile terrain, illness and lack of food. Retracing their steps, they eventually reached Chambers Creek again in August 1860 and from there returned to Adelaide. They had done extremely well, the passing of the centre of the continent having been an added bonus, yet still they had not solved the south-to-north conundrum. To make matters worse, Stuart now had competition in the form of Burke and Wills. He would have to try again.

With a little persuasion, the South Australian government backed the new mission which left in January 1860. This time Stuart also had a small armed escort to help protect him from the aboriginal attacks that had dogged his previous mission. Consequently, it was a relatively large expedition, its numbers eventually settling at nine men, forty horses and a load including six months' supplies. Within three months they had reached Stuart's previous northern record but now came the same problem of trying to conquer the almost impossible terrain that had forced Stuart to retreat on the previous occasion. After several false starts, Stuart's party eventually progressed northwards as far as what is now known as Newcastle Waters. They were into uncharted territory again, but once more it was so difficult to traverse that it halted the mission in its tracks. Time after time Stuart scouted for routes through and around the hostile terrain to no avail. Furthermore, supplies as ever were starting to run low and they were now being attacked again by aborigines. It was no good. They would have to once more return home, defeated, where Stuart would soon learn of the disappearance of the advance party of Burke and Will's competitor expedition. He did not know it at the time, but the now deceased men had already beaten him across the continent, even if they had not managed to return. In spite of the rivalry, Stuart was still sufficiently moved to offer to find the missing men, although other searches already under way made this unnecessary.

So, with the south-to-north goal still unobtained as far as Stuart was aware, and with no help required in the Burke and Wills search, he decided that the only course of action he could now take was to turn around and head north again to finish the job he had started. After literally just a few weeks to rest and prepare, Stuart had gathered even more men and horses together, albeit with much sparser government support this time, and he was on the march again in October 1861. In April 1862 Stuart attained his previous furthest-north position, again encountering hostile aborigines on top of the hostile terrain. This time, though, he would not be defeated. It took several more flawed attempts before he finally found a way forward and the group were marking new routes again. This breakthrough made, they pressed on through more difficult land and tough conditions to finally reach the north coast, in July 1862.

Stuart's goal was now to return home safely and achieve something Burke and Wills had been unable to duplicate. Although he knew his route, the party had limited rations and Stuart above all was in the worst condition, scurvy taking as much out of him as starvation. He had to be carried part of the way back and, on several occasions, it was feared that Stuart might suffer the same fate as Burke and Wills. But he pulled through, the rest of the team successfully persevering too, and together they returned to Adelaide in triumph in January 1863.

Stuart had not only managed to go one step better than Burke and Wills, his route across Australia also proved to be the more practical one for the long-sought-after telegraph line from India across the continent from Darwin to the south. Within a decade it had been constructed, its path virtually mirroring the explorers' footsteps, as does the Stuart Highway from Adelaide to Darwin today.

The establishment of the telegraph line and its stations in Stuart's wake across the centre of the continent also opened up the possibility of detailed searches of many parts of Western Australia for the first time. Although Edward Eyre had traversed the region between 1840 and 1841 he had been forced to stick close to the south coast. John Forrest, who later went on to become the first Premier of Western Australia, had repeated this feat in the opposite direction in 1870, but now he sought to cross to Western Australia through its centre. He succeeded in 1874, leaving from Geraldton and eventually reaching the Peaks overland telegraph station in September of that year. He had, however, already been beaten in the race to become the first to find a desert route. Ernest Giles and William Gosse, who was the first European to see Uluru, had both tried already and failed, but a party under Peter Warburton and John Lewis was more fortunate. They had set out from Alice Springs in 1873 and, even though Warburton was sixty years old, eventually managed to reach Roebourne on the coast.

By this time, though, the man whose achievements had forged the way for the telegraph line as well as for the explorers who followed him was already being overlooked. The Burke and Wills episode would forever catch the attention of historians in preference to Stuart's exploits and by now the little Scot was no longer alive to remind people of his achievements. Indeed, he had never really recovered from the ways in which his health was compromised during his expeditions. In 1864 he had returned to Britain to convalesce, having to survive on an insufficient pension from the South Australian government. Although the Royal Geographical Society had supported him with the award of two medals during his lifetime and had lobbied on his behalf for more income, it would all largely be futile; Stuart died in June 1866. Large parts of Australia's interior were finally on the map but, like Burke and Wills, the explorer who was responsible for placing them there had to all intents paid the ultimate price.

Chapter 10
ALL AROUND THE WORLD:
The Circumnavigators

Christopher Columbus (*see* page 105) knew the world was round. Long before him, the ancient Greeks had come to the same conclusion, based on a number of observations, not least of which was the fact that the topsails were the first part of a ship one saw when the ship appeared on the horizon. This would only happen, they reasoned, if the world were in fact a globe, and not flat.

Yet, frustratingly, by the start of the sixteenth century, nobody had managed to sail all the way around the globe. While this state of affairs persisted, then, no matter how many learned people insisted that the world was in fact a sphere and not a square or a disc or, indeed, even a cylinder, the fear persisted, particularly among sailors, that if one sailed too far, one would simply drop off the end.

So it was perhaps inevitable that sooner or later someone would overcome their vertigo and be brave enough to explicitly set out to 'circumnavigate' or voyage around the earth. The adventurer who did this would rightly earn a place in history as having completed one of the greatest exploratory feats of all time. Yet even for the most determined of captains it was no easy task. Three-quarters of the world's surface is covered in water, but land, most notably America, kept on getting in the way of attempts to circumnavigate. Any explorer who was to achieve this goal would have to be smart enough to find a way around the New World first.

Once this was finally achieved during the sixteenth century, however, the fascination of travellers with the concept of circumnavigation did not end there.

Indeed, sailing around the world continued to appeal to adventurers and their public alike as a worthy end for its own sake. And even though it had finally been rounded, much of its surface still remained undiscovered. Which is why, even into the nineteenth century, 'circumnavigators' could continue to stimulate the public interest as long as they found something new or achieved something hitherto unaccomplished on their way round.

Indeed, some circumnavigators discovered so much during their global travels that their feats could not possibly be recorded under any other category. James Cook, for example, sits in this chapter for that reason. Yes, he circumnavigated, but ironically that was not his major achievement. He simply saw and discovered so much during his global travels that he could not be given full justice in any other section. In a way, though, even Cook was standing on the shoulders of giants. For there was a time before his comprehensive accomplishments that the very concept of circumnavigation was a worthy goal in its own right.

Which conveniently brings the story back to the early sixteenth century and the earliest globe trotters.

Ferdinand Magellan *(c.1480–1521)*

The first man to be credited with leading an expedition that sailed around the world did not, in fact, complete the voyage himself. He was dead long before the mission was finished. So too were the majority of his original crew of more than two hundred. Yet, crucially, three years after the fleet had set out, one ship of the five that had left Spain in 1519 limped home with a paltry eighteen men on board, having rounded the globe. So, in spite of the losses, shipwrecks and the absence of it's leader, the legend of Ferdinand Magellan's great voyage of circumnavigation was born.

The thirty-six months of the party's time at sea brought a compelling story of discovery, desperation, mutiny and success on a scale perhaps only fitting to such a ground-breaking voyage. Endless hardships and a whole ocean of unknowns were bound to bring drama and discontent in equal measure. Yet from privation came salvation for the very lucky few who at last returned home in September 1522, their place amongst the greats in the history of exploration secure.

Even the preparations for the voyage had a whiff of scandal surrounding them. Ferdinand Magellan was actually born a Portuguese citizen, the non-anglicised version of his name being Fernão de Magalhães. Young Fernão had spent much of his early career serving with the Portuguese navy in India and the Far East, so the known route from Europe to Asia around the base of Africa was already familiar to him. Some had speculated on the possibility of reaching these lands, particularly the much-prized Moluccas or 'Spice Islands', via an alternative route. Although a passage round the Americas had yet to be found, it had been speculated that Asia would soon be within its discoverer's grasp if it existed. From there, a circumnavigation through the known waters of the Far East and Africa could be completed. But speculation was one thing: few were brave enough to actively attempt this crossing.

Ferdinand Magellan was, nonetheless, keen. Unfortunately, his king, Dom Manuel, was not. Indeed, he actively disliked Magellan to the point where the sailor abandoned his Portuguese citizenship and marched off with his plan to Portugal's arch-rivals, the Spanish.

King Charles I of Spain was much more interested in Magellan's ideas. As well as the possibility of a shorter route to Asia, the discovery of new lands and the undoubted kudos associated with sponsoring the first circumnavigation of the globe, there was an added political attraction to such a voyage. Both Portugal and Spain had agreed to abide by an earlier papal ruling that the former had first claim on new lands discovered to the east of an imaginary line drawn 370 leagues west of the Cape Verde Islands. The latter had rights on land to the west. But if the world were to be circumnavigated, sooner or later these two domains would meet. By the same logic, if Spain reached Asia, in particular the Spice Islands, by sailing west from Europe, then she could begin making claims on its wealth in favour of Portugal or any others. So the former Portuguese sailor was reborn Hernando de Magallanes, the Spanish version of his name, and told to prepare a fleet to sail around the world.

Portugal was appalled at this perceived treachery. She made efforts to scupper the mission through secret attempts to sabotage the fleet's supplies. Many of the senior Spanish crew who would accompany the ships were little more impressed. Unhappy at the prospect of being led by a Portuguese native, they were hatching plans to murder Magellan at sea before they had even departed. The sniff of mutiny was already in the air.

Nonetheless, Magellan's five vessels, the *San Antonio*, the *Concepcion*, the *Santiago*, the *Trinidad* and the *Victoria* departed from Spain on 20 September, 1519. They made their way across the Atlantic over the next three months, eventually arriving at Rio de Janeiro where they rested and took more supplies on board. Magellan's plan was to head south from here and investigate every possible opening that might provide a passage through to Balboa's 'South Sea' (*see* page 123). For all they knew one did not even exist. Indeed, many speculated that the South American continent simply continued all the way to the South Pole. Even if it did not, any channel might prove to be practically un-navigable, as would be the case with the Northwest Passage around North America.

Magellan pressed on south in accordance with his plan. Openings were investigated, but continually disappointed as bays or rivers. Autumn arrived and many of the crew wanted to land for the winter while the party was still in reasonably temperate climes. Yet as Magellan pushed on, and the temperatures grew ever colder and the weather more hostile, mutiny threatened again. By the time Magellan at last conceded defeat to the elements for the season, and they docked for the winter, they were in the bitter climate of southern Argentina. Some of the men could take no more and at last the threatened subversion broke out into open hostility as mutinous crews and officers alike demanded they retreat. Magellan, however, was having none of it. In a daring display of bravado, he outmanoeuvred the rebels controlling three of the five ships and executed their three ringleaders. Two others were later abandoned at their winter quarters as punishment.

Little improved, however. As winter began receding, the *Santiago* left the main group to scout further ahead, only succeeding in running aground. The crew were saved, but the ship was a wreck.

Spring arrived, and the remaining four vessels continued south in search of a passage. Many still persisted in trying to persuade Magellan to head home, or at least change direction and sail instead around Africa's known southern tip, but the leader pressed on.

Another potential opening was spotted towards the end of October 1520, and two ships were sent to investigate. As they did so, however, a fierce storm blew up. The ships disappeared from view as all hands fought the elements and Magellan feared that they too would be wrecked. A few days later, though, after the storm had at last subsided, the two vessels returned in triumph. From their probing, tidal observations and the salty water in the passage they had been able to ascertain that it almost certainly provided a way through to the 'South Sea'. They were right: they had discovered what would be known to generations thereafter as the Straits of Magellan, a route around the southern tip of America.

The news was good, but Magellan's luck was no better. As they sailed through the passage, they again had to constantly battle the elements to avoid running aground. Furthermore, the *San Antonio* took advantage of the confusion brought about by the conditions to take the opportunity to this time successfully desert. She was carrying a disproportionate amount of supplies, which meant that the crew would be even worse off during the next, probably most challenging, leg of their journey. In spite of everything, though, the three remaining vessels made it through the Straits by the end of November and finally entered much calmer waters on the other side. Magellan consequently re-christened Balboa's 'South Sea' the 'Pacific', a name for the world's largest ocean that would endure.

Magellan did not appreciate, however, just quite how large this body of water would be. He set a course northwest and anticipated being at the Spice Islands within a few days. Yet, apart from one short stop at a tiny Pacific island, it would be nearly a hundred days before he encountered land again, a duration for which the ships' supplies, particularly after the San Antonio desertion, were not in any way equipped. Men, many men, started to die. Those who survived were reduced to eating anything that was vaguely edible from maggots to leather to sawdust.

Incredibly, though, all three ships made the crossing and in March they landed at what is now known as the island of Guam. Encountering some resistance, they stopped only long enough to replenish their supplies, but at least they now had sufficient food and water to survive their onward journey. A few days later they arrived at one of the Philippine islands and were thrilled at its abundance of food and fertile grounds. The temptation to linger was too great, and they did, but it was a decision that would cost Magellan his life.

The party spent several weeks moving from island to island within the Philippine archipelago, gorging on its profusion and enjoying the hospitality of largely friendly natives. Indeed, Magellan's purpose there was not only hedonistic but also spiritual, as he set about converting the inhabitants of the islands to Christianity. For the most part, the locals were amenable to his overtures and embraced the new religion. Yet there was also some dissent and it was the over-confident manner in which Magellan confronted this opposition that would result in his downfall.

The leader of the people on the small island of Mactan, who would come to be known as Lapu Lapu, flatly refused to bow to Magellan's demands. Magellan decided to teach him a lesson and confronted the Filipino and his large band of supporters with a small troop of Spanish soldiers. The Europeans struggled in their heavy armour as they waded into battle in the shallow waters off Mactan. Although the fight took some time to unfold, they were eventually overwhelmed. Magellan was targeted, overpowered and cut down, a sight that sent the remnants of his little army fleeing back to their ships. It was April 27 1521. The man whom history would credit with leading the first circumnavigation of the world had died when only half-way around it.

A supporter of the earlier mutiny, Juan Sebastian Del Cano, now took control of the remaining men and ships. There was simply not enough of the crew left to man three vessels, so the *Concepcion* was abandoned. The remainder of the party did eventually make it to the Spice Islands after which they decided to head home in opposite directions to improve the chances of one of the vessels avoiding capture by the Portuguese or succumbing to the seas. The *Trinidad* did not make it but the *Victoria*, which had opted to head home via Africa, was successful. Nonetheless, the ship was in such a bad state after its long voyage home and so low on supplies that it had to call in at the Cape Verde Islands on the way back. There, the Portuguese captured a number of its crew, such that merely eighteen men, including Del Cano, finally returned to Spain, barely managing to keep the *Victoria* afloat, in September 1522.

Only these few survivors had circumnavigated the world. Fortunately, the writer Antonio Francesca Pigafetta, who had been secretly keeping a journal of the voyage, was also among them. His writings formed the basis of subsequent generations' knowledge of the trip, one of the greatest feats, and most dramatic of tales, in the chronicles of exploration.

Sir Francis Drake *(c.1540–1596)*

If the Spanish could circumnavigate the world, then the English were confident that their maritime men would also be equal to the task. Indeed, by the 1570s, Queen Elizabeth I of England was becoming increasingly frustrated and jealous of the Spanish supremacy in the New World. Together with the Portuguese in Brazil, not to mention Africa and Asia, the two southern European nations were dominating the flow of global trade into Europe, siphoning off for themselves all the additional treasures that came with owning remote colonies. It was time to do something about it. So, in 1577, Sir Francis Drake was sent out on his own circumnavigation attempt.

Secrecy surrounded the mission. Drake would after all be sailing through potentially hostile Spanish and Portuguese waters. Even more confidentiality was ascribed to the true hidden agenda of the expedition: the plunder of Spanish ships and settlements to bring back treasure to England. Such actions were risky, especially if they were seen to be endorsed by the Queen and not as the lone deeds of a renegade buccaneer. It could easily bring the country to war with the Spanish. But there was a world to win with vast wealth at stake, and Drake and Elizabeth alike were prepared to gamble.

So 165 men left England in December 1577 aboard five vessels; the *Pelican*, the *Swan*, the *Christopher*, the *Marigold* and the *Elizabeth*. Such was the clandestine nature of the mission that even many of the men on board were not made aware of its intended course until it was already under way. Passing by the coast of Africa and the Cape Verde Islands, Drake reached the South American continent at Brazil in April 1578. He set his course south with a view to rounding the tip of the continent in the manner Magellan had achieved half a century before.

Already, though, the voyage was beset with difficulties and hardships, just as Magellan had found. One of the early decisions Drake had to take on arriving in America was to abandon two of his ships, which were already struggling to remain seaworthy. Thus, he continued his drift south with only the *Pelican*, the *Marigold* and the *Elizabeth*. In another duplication of Magellan, Drake had to quell an attempted mutiny: the execution of its ringleader Thomas Doughty soon put an end to the rebellion.

In an effort to put the uncertain start and bad feeling

behind him, Drake relaunched his expedition. He sought to stir all his men to their nation's cause and symbolically renamed the *Pelican* the *Golden Hind*. In August 1578, they entered the Straits of Magellan. Unlike their namesake's earlier voyage, the passage of the Straits proved fairly straightforward, completed in just over two weeks. Drake's problems began when they entered the Pacific. Storms blew up and for weeks the three vessels struggled to make progress. In the end they became separated. The *Marigold* was sunk with no survivors. The *Elizabeth*, having been unable to find the *Golden Hind* again, eventually gave up and returned home. In the confusion, Drake himself ended up sufficiently far south to prove that the 'Tierra del Fuego' off the southern tip of South America was, in fact, an island and not the headland, as many had suspected, of an undiscovered southern continent, *Terra Australis*.

Drake soon came to realise that he was now down to one vessel, yet he pressed on unperturbed. Still his luck did not improve. Drake's first landfall on the western side of South America brought him into an immediate conflict with the locals which nearly stopped the expedition in its remaining tracks. Nonetheless, the *Golden Hind* persisted up the Latin American coastline and, at last, the long desired rewards were forthcoming.

Even though he possessed only a single ship and a limited number of men, Drake found he could plunder and pick off Spanish vessels and settlements along the coastline almost as he pleased. Treasure, especially silver by the ton, was wrenched from the unprepared hands of the Spanish and hoarded aboard the increasingly laden *Golden Hind*. For the best part of six months, Drake indulged in an orgy of ill-gotten gains before escaping out of sight of his pursuers into the waters of North America.

At this point it is possible that Drake began searching for a Northwest Passage from the Pacific side. If such a channel could have been found, it would have been the crowning glory of his mission, opening up an all-English trade route to Asia. He almost certainly went as far north as the present-day Canadian border in its pursuit but was ultimately disappointed. Nevertheless, he made harbour somewhere along the North American coastline, possibly at California, where he christened the surrounding lands 'New Albion' and took possession of them on behalf of England. It would be another supporting claim to

England's ongoing assertions regarding North America. Indeed, Drake got on so well with the natives here that he stayed for over five weeks and they declared him to be their new king.

Duty called, however, for the Englishman. It was time to take his booty home. In late July 1579, he decided to head west to avoid Spanish revenge attempts, a route that had the added attraction of augmenting his fame through the completion of what would be a circumnavigation. In around two months he crossed the Pacific, after which time he visited a number of islands in south-eastern Asia, establishing potential trading partnerships. In November he made it to the Moluccas and soon he was laden with spices as well. This period was not without incident, however. In December he grounded on a reef, but eventually was released and managed to escape with only minimal damage to the *Golden Hind*.

In March 1580, Drake made a conscious decision to continue in earnest on his voyage back to England. He rounded the southern tip of Africa in June, and by September he received a hero's welcome as he finally returned to England at Plymouth harbour. The Queen was delighted with his success. Drake had claimed new territory for the Crown, matched the Spanish in circumnavigating the world and, more importantly, he had brought home a ship full of 'their' treasure. Risking the wrath of Spain even further, Elizabeth knighted the man who England's rivals considered to be nothing more than a common pirate.

Drake's circumnavigation was certainly a tremendous feat and, as with Magellan, another tale of exploration full of the highest drama. Yet, while it was probably the Englishman's greatest achievement, it was by no means his only one in a career littered with highlights. Even before he set off on the circumnavigation, he had made exploratory history. In 1572 he had crossed the Isthmus of Panama and became the first Englishman to view the Pacific Ocean. This was shortly after he had plundered the nearby Spanish settlement at Nombre de Dios and, once more, he returned to England laden with booty. Earlier in his career, he had similarly been a thorn in Spanish sides during raids off Panama and the West Indies.

Indeed, Spain would come to resent Drake more and more. In 1585, he ran riot amongst Spanish settlements in the West Indies. In 1587, during a daring raid, he sailed into the harbour at Cádiz, and set ablaze a large part of the Spanish fleet that was docked there in preparation for a full-scale invasion of England. When the attack came a year later in the form of the Spanish Armada, it was Drake who was pivotal in repulsing the invaders, chasing them all the way up the English Channel and beyond.

Drake would continue irritating the Spanish until the very end of his days. From 1595–96 he was back in the West Indies doing his best to disrupt Spanish settlements once again when he fell ill. Eventually, in January 1596, he succumbed to his disease, and the man who had been master of the sea – around the globe – was laid to rest in her waters.

James Cook *(1728–1779)*

Egged on by Drake's example, circumnavigation increasingly became seen as something eminently achievable, given enough determination. The Englishman Thomas Cavendish quickly followed in Drake's footsteps with his own round-the-world repeat of his compatriot's voyage from 1586–88. Drake would no doubt have been pleased to learn that Cavendish, too, wreaked havoc amongst the Spanish shipping around South America. Just over a decade later, the Dutch took their place among the globe's circumnavigators. Their ground-breaking expedition was led by Olivier van Noort between 1598 and 1601. Even he could not resist having a go at a number of Spanish vessels and settlements as he sailed past Chile and Peru.

So by the 1760s, over a century and a half later, circumnavigation was certainly no longer a novel concept. Nevertheless, James Cook, who began his first round-the-world voyage in this decade, still came to be regarded as one of the greatest circumnavigators of all time. Not merely because he circled the globe – twice – but simply because of the vast range of territories he visited and, in many instances, discovered. Indeed, his achievements would become an inspiration to generations of explorers who followed in his wake.

Perhaps what makes Cook's career all the more impressive is that in an age where being born into wealth or the upper classes was usually essential to any kind of meaningful progress, the English captain started life with no social advantages whatsoever. He was the son of a labourer, one of seven siblings who grew up in a rural Yorkshire village where education was limited. At seventeen, he was apprenticed to a shipping firm in

Whitby. He gained his sea-legs over the next decade, transporting coal aboard ships off England's east coast. When he joined the navy at the age of twenty-seven, he nevertheless had to start again at the very bottom of its career ladder, in spite of this sea experience. Cook knuckled down to the task with the same determined spirit that he had shown in improving his own education through self-teaching during his time at Whitby. Consequently, his career quickly progressed. After an early tour of duty off North America, he was soon entrusted with important surveying work. For this task he had a natural flair, and several years of charting off Newfoundland and the subsequent maps he produced only continued to augment Cook's reputation.

Nevertheless, it was still a surprise to many when Cook was entrusted to lead the important *Endeavour* expedition to the Pacific in 1768. For Cook himself, though, it was the opportunity to prove that his faith in his own ability was well placed. He subsequently excelled.

The expedition was, in name at least, a scientific one. Venus was due to make a passing before the sun in June 1769 and the British were keen to make scientific studies of the crossing from several locations. Cook's job was to establish an observation post on the newly-discovered island of Tahiti in the Pacific. The *Endeavour*, carrying Cook, his crew and a team of scientists, set out from England in August 1768 for the long journey to the other side of the world via South America. Within three months they had reached Brazil and early in the new year they had rounded the southern tip of America. By April, they were in Tahiti itself in plenty of time to make their preparations for Venus's crossing. This event, and Cook's subsequent charting of the coastline of Tahiti, would not, however, turn out to be the main highlights of the voyage.

On leaving England, Cook had been handed an envelope with instructions not to open it until the Tahiti portion of the expedition was completed. When he finally did so, it revealed a truly exciting return mission. He was being asked to seek out or disprove the existence of the suspected, but unfound, great southern land known as *Terra Australis*. Cook set about fulfilling his duty.

Initially, he would be disappointed, the southern winter hampering his progress towards the bottom of the world to such an extent that he was forced to retreat to New Zealand, having seen no sign of the sought-after continent. This resulted, however, in the beginning of Cook's long fabled association with Australasia. First of all, though, he became the first to circumnavigate and fully map New Zealand before moving on to Australia itself. The east coast of the great continent was still unexplored and uncharted and it was James Cook who would unveil it. Much to his surprise, and that of many others, he found a lush, fertile and habitable coastline in contrast to much of the known, barren shorelines in other parts of Australia.

In April 1770, they landed in Botany Bay (now in Sydney), so called because of the wealth of new wildlife discovered in the area. Indeed, Joseph Banks, who would go on to become the famous President of the Royal Society, largely made his name as a ground-breaking botanist within Cook's team on the back of these Australian landings. Shortly afterwards, the party discovered Sydney harbour, then proceeded up the rest of the Australian east coast, navigating the hazardous Great Barrier Reef which, at one point, very nearly wrecked them. On the homeward journey, Cook confirmed that New Guinea and Australia were indeed separate landmasses by sailing through the previously reported Torres Strait. Illness, probably malaria, struck the crew in what is now Indonesia, where they stopped on the way back in October, and a number of men died. Nevertheless, the mission was considered a huge success when Cook finally arrived home in July 1771, his first circumnavigation of the world completed after routing via the southern tip of Africa. As well as the scientific gains and discoveries, Cook had claimed New Zealand and the east coast of Australia for England.

If anyone had doubted Cook's capabilities before his first voyage, then few would be questioning his appointment at the head of another mammoth expedition only a year later. On his first circumnavigation, Cook's instructions had directed him to prove or disprove the existence of a supposed southern continent at even deeper latitudes. He had been unable to solve this question conclusively so the Royal Society sponsored another expedition to find out and Cook was appointed at its head, even though he personally had doubts about whether any such land existed.

Nonetheless, Cook left England aboard the *Resolution* in July 1772, this time accompanied by a second vessel, the *Adventure*, headed by Tobias Furneaux. Their outward journey took them via the southern tip of Africa, from where they continued southwards in pursuit of their goal. In January 1773, Cook became the first ever explorer to cross the Antarctic Circle, but no land was sighted. Worst still he was separated from the *Adventure*, which eventually made its way home without Cook, after stopping at New Zealand. In March, Cook was forced to retreat to New Zealand himself, from where he would launch another attempt to find *Terra Australis*. Again unsuccessful, Cook this time headed to Tahiti, went on to map some of the Tongan islands and then, towards the end of 1773, had another go at the south. In January 1774, he reached a furthest south record of 71 degrees 10 minutes, but still the ice thwarted him before he could see the Antarctic continent. Cook retreated to the Pacific in March 1774. He spent the last months of his time in the ocean exploring, mapping and sometimes discovering Pacific islands, before moving on to complete the first eastward circumnavigation of the globe by heading home via South America. On the way back, he also discovered and claimed South Georgia and the South Sandwich Islands for Britain.

The Englishman arrived home in July 1775, having

proved that no new southern continent existed above polar latitudes. Even though he had found no evidence of it, Cook conceded that it was possible that land might exist further south, buried in amongst the swathes of ice but, to all intents and purposes, it would be useless. That opinion closed off almost all Antarctic speculation and, certainly, further exploration for the next half century. As well as 'conclusively' ending the *Terra Australis* debate, other features of this voyage were that again Cook had managed to stave off scurvy (as he had done on his first expedition), through a diet including fresh fruits, vegetables and meat wherever possible The cause of the disease was still unknown and it usually debilitated crews on long voyages at this time. He had also kept other diseases at bay through a strict routine of hygienic practices and cleaning. Furthermore, Cook's second voyage carried John Harrison's revolutionary H4 chronometer which, for the first time, provided a consistently accurate longitude reading, the lack of which had long been the bane of naval navigators' lives.

In spite of overtures being made to him regarding some kind of retirement following his global successes, Cook could not be kept on land for long. The man who had circumnavigated westwards, circumnavigated eastwards, rounded New Zealand, discovered eastern Australia, entered the Antarctic and unveiled countless Pacific and other islands was now set on finding the long-sought Northwest Passage. It was, after all, one of the few remaining challenges left open to him. So, within a year, with the technology of the day at his disposal, Cook was on the seas again.

Once more Cook captained the *Resolution*, this time accompanied by the *Discovery* headed by Captain Charles Clerke. They left in July 1776, voyaging round Africa and on to New Zealand. From there, Cook moved further into the Pacific again, discovering yet more landfall including the Hawaiian islands in 1778. His next target was the western coast of North America, which he comprehensively mapped from California into Alaska. He continued northwards, penetrating the Bering Strait but quickly become bogged down by ice. Despite repeated attempts to find a passage around North America from this eastern avenue he could not make headway, so he retreated to Hawaii. It would prove a fateful decision. Although initially welcomed by the natives there – Cook was at first thought to be some kind of god – relations soon became strained. In February 1779, Cook took leave of the islands but, after a few days at sea, storms damaged his ships and he was forced to return to Hawaii. The Englishmen and their local hosts soon began squabbling, however, and during a fracas that consequently broke out, Cook was killed.

James Cook was an explorer in the truest sense of the word. He never tired of surveying new territory, travelling to previously unseen lands or attempting to better the feats of those who had lived before him. From an unprivileged beginning he had risen to famous heights though his own determination and ability to become, arguably, the greatest circumnavigator of all. Yet it was this same drive that had resulted in him rejecting retirement so that he could once more try to answer an unsolved question of exploration. To a man such as this, the lure of the unknown was a temptation impossible to resist. Curiosity ended up killing Cook.

Chapter 11

FURTHER, HIGHER, DEEPER:
Extremities

Some explorers have found new continents, some have traversed the polar regions and some have sailed around the world. What all of these explorers had in common is that they were typically seeking to discover new territory or geographical features, or they were quite simply looking for a quicker way to get from A to B.

Later, however, came a new breed of explorers who knew what existed, knew very definitely the goals they were chasing and literally the size of the task in front of them. These were the men and women who pursued the 'extremities'. The top of the world, the bottom of the world, seeking to land on objects out of this world; these were the goals the new adventurers prized. They were very different objectives from those sought by the centuries of explorers who had come before them, but they were no less worthy and, in many ways, even more tantalising.

The climbers who attempted to scale the world's highest mountain could see their target before them. So too could the space explorers seeking to reach the moon. The exact distance that would have to be travelled to reach the ocean's lowest point, and its precise location, were already known to the underwater voyagers who wanted to be the first to land there. Yet this prior knowledge only made the task of being the one to conquer these targets all the more exciting, and frustrating, as challengers came ever closer but ultimately failed.

In the end, though, determination and persistence would finally lead to success for the chosen few. And so the twentieth century's great exploratory goals of peaks, troughs and outer space were also ticked off the ever dwindling checklist of 'famous firsts'.

Here are the victors, quite literally, in the extreme.

Sir Edmund Hillary *(born 1919)*

'We did not know if it was humanly possible to reach the top of Mount Everest,' said Sir Edmund Hillary, recalling his remarkable climb to the roof of the world. Yet at 11.30 a.m. on 29 May 1953, the New Zealander, along with his Sherpa guide, Tenzing Norgay, became the first man to record such an achievement. Fortunately, on reaching the summit, they did not 'drop dead or something of that nature', as Hillary had earlier feared. Instead, they returned safely to lower heights as world famous heroes. They were, after all, the men who had stood higher than any before them.

Mount Everest had long been regarded as the 'Third Pole'. Unlike the North and South Poles, that were reached early in the twentieth century, 'Chomolungma', as Tenzing's people knew the world's highest mountain, had remained stubbornly unconquered. Indeed, fifteen previous expeditions had tried and failed to reach the summit, some failing to return at all, including the 1924 venture that killed George Leigh Mallory and his companion Andrew Irvine.

Mallory had been involved in three attempts on Everest before the great peak claimed him as one of its many victims. Given that he was climbing over thirty years before Hillary, using much more primitive technology and with no supplementary oxygen at all during his first two attempts, he came tantalisingly close to his goal. During his initial 'reconnaissance' mission on the mountain in 1921, he identified its north face as the most likely route to the top. A year later, he returned and surpassed 27,000 feet, a new world mountaineering record by a significant margin and only 2,000 feet from the summit of Everest. Unfortunately, seven Sherpa guides were killed in an avalanche during the 1922 attempt as Mallory tried to push on even higher.

Nevertheless, he returned in 1924 and, striking out from the main party's base camp with the twenty-two year old Irvine, had soon reached similar heights. Indeed, there remains some speculation even now over whether the Britons might have actually conquered Everest on this final journey before perishing on their return.

They were last sighted on 8 June by a member of the support team following behind them. They were scaling a formidable rock obstacle known as the 'Second Step'. As they progressed towards the summit, cloud moved in. The weather turned and it was this misfortune that probably cost the two climbers their lives, either before or after they made it to the top.

Given the difficulties in overcoming the Second Step and completing the ascent on Everest's north face, however, especially without specialist equipment, it is more likely that Mallory and Irvine did not reach the summit before perishing. Even the discovery of Mallory's frozen corpse in 1999 offered little further evidence to suggest that they made it, although the camera the men were carrying, which might contain conclusive images, remained unfound.

Subsequent attempts by others probably came even nearer. Only a year before Hillary's eventual success, a Swiss expedition had reached Everest's South Peak and come frustratingly close to its summit before being forced to turn back. Tellingly, Tenzing Norgay had also been a member of that party, accompanying the climber Raymond Lambert to within 1,000 feet of the top, a then 'known' record. This experience, along with five previously unsuccessful attempts, would be an important factor in the Sherpa's full ascent with Hillary a year later. 'I needed to go', Tenzing said. 'The pull of Everest was stronger for me than any force on earth.'

Hillary was no less determined to succeed where others had failed in the following year. 'I think motivation is the single most important factor in any success,' he later said. 'In the field of exploration it is the thing that makes the difference between someone who does really well and someone who does not.' To this end, he completed eleven climbs of other Himalayan mountains above 20,000 feet as part of his preparation for Everest. Prior to that he had undertaken ascents in both the European and New Zealand Alps, where he had initially developed his passion for climbing.

It was these earlier Himalayan adventures that brought Hillary to the attention of the then Colonel (later Lord) John Hunt. He was organising the 1953 British team's assault on Everest and both Hillary and Tenzing were invited to join the squad. Both accepted.

The climb began well. In May 1953, Hunt's men matched the Swiss team's earlier achievement by reaching Everest's South Peak. By this point, though, the high altitude and demanding ascent had taken its physical toll on most of the party. Only Hillary and Tenzing were strong enough to continue and so it was they who set off at dawn on 29 May 1953 to walk their way into history. The final ascent was by no means straightforward, however. They had to scale unforgiving walls of ice and rock, a task made no easier by faulty oxygen bottles. With limited air supply and arduous terrain their progress at times became tortuously slow, but inch by inch they closed in on the roof of the world.

At last they arrived. On reaching the peak, Hillary took the now famous photograph of Tenzing on the summit, which was soon splashed on the front pages of newspapers around the world. Their success coincided with the coronation of Britain's Queen Elizabeth the second, who was to knight Hillary and award Tenzing the George medal.

After decades of expeditions attempting to reach the top, Hillary and Tenzing spent only fifteen minutes at the summit. 'There came no feeling of extreme pleasure or excitement', said Hillary, 'more a sense of quiet satisfaction, and even a bit of a surprise.' His attention was focused on completing their equally dangerous descent before the enormity of their achievement could truly take hold.

Perhaps the most remarkable aspect of Hillary's story is the humility he retained in the face of world fame. He maintains that he was merely a 'competent amateur' in spite of the fact that he also went on to become part of the first team since 1912 to reach the South Pole over land during a 1957–58 expedition, and climbed Mount Herschel in Alaska in 1967. In 1977, only two years after the devastating loss of his wife, Louise, and youngest daughter, Belinda, in a plane crash in Nepal, he completed an expedition up the Ganges river from its end to its Himalayan source.

Furthermore, Hillary did not forget the land that had been the source of his fame. His close friendship with Tenzing, and the time he spent with the Sherpa people, saw him draw attention to the poverty in which much of the population of Nepal were forced to live. From the 1960s onwards the New Zealander became involved in fundraising and implementing projects to build schools, hospitals and other buildings in a cause that would occupy much of his time for the remainder of his life.

Such activities, along with Hillary's famous expeditions, were a far cry from the small world of Tuakau, Auckland, where he had grown up as a boy. Beginning his working life as a simple beekeeper, he had no idea of the achievements that would later follow. 'All I knew', said Hillary, 'was that I wanted to get involved in adventurous activity.'

Jacques Ernest Jean Piccard *(1922–2008)*

From the top of the world to the bottom of it. While mankind had been busy for centuries unveiling everything above sea-level, much of what lay below it remained a mystery. Even today work continues in this area. Certainly it was well into the twentieth century, as with the ascent to the summit of Everest, before the deepest point on earth was conquered. That honour belonged to Jacques Ernest Jean Piccard in 1960.

Only decades earlier, descents into just a few hundred feet of water were virtually unthinkable. The extreme pressures involved and the absence of flexible breathing equipment made underwater exploration a virtual non-entity. A British expedition led by George Nares in the 1870s, who was also later involved in an unsuccessful

North Pole attempt (*see* page 220), did spend several years mapping the peaks and troughs of the sea beds of the world's major oceans. Yet the team had no way of actually seeing the underwater world they had been able to chart from the surface. It would only be a major step change in marine technology during the twentieth century that would finally open up this mysterious domain. Jacques Piccard himself was at the forefront of this revolution.

In fact, early forms of submarine technology had been in existence since the seventeenth century. The wooden device invented by Dutchman Cornelius van Drebel, however, could only manage depths of a few feet and was in no way suited to any kind of meaningful exploration. The concept would gradually be improved, but it would not be until the invention of the bathysphere in the 1930s that the equipment required for deep-sea investigation began to emerge. William Beebe and Otis Barton descended over three thousand feet in their purpose-built device, a pressurized steel globe that would be lowered into the ocean on a wire from a ship.

In 1943 Jacques Cousteau, perhaps the most famous underwater adventurer of all time, made another breakthrough. Together with French compatriot Emile Gagnan, he designed the aqualung. This portable breathing device meant that for the first time divers could stay submerged for extended periods and still have the flexibility to easily move around, opening up a whole new world of underwater exploratory possibilities to a new generation of investigators. Indeed, through his books, films and television documentaries, Cousteau brought the marine world to millions on the surface who, for the first time, could begin to fully appreciate what lurked below.

Yet for all its assistance in general underwater exploration, Cousteau's invention was no use to those who wanted to penetrate to the very bottom of the seas. This challenge would be left to the Piccard family, although it was not initially led by Jacques but by his father Auguste. The older Piccard was a physicist from Switzerland who had earlier achieved the record for the greatest height – some 50,000 feet – ascended in a balloon (of his own design) in the early 1930s. His attentions now turned in the opposite direction, though, and in 1948 Auguste unveiled his invention, a 'bathyscaphe' which improved on the earlier deep-sea plunging machines. Jacques assisted his father with the design and preparations and its first unmanned test successfully reached a depth of more than four and a half thousand feet. The platform for an assault on the bottom of the world was emerging at last.

The Piccards sought to improve on their vessel, bringing out new models in 1953 and 1954. The later of these achieved another record depth, this time of over 10,000 feet, in the Mediterranean Sea. More investment and a team of scientists were required, however, to make the breakthrough needed to reach the more than 35,000 feet that the world's deepest known underwater point descended to. In 1958, therefore, the US Navy stepped in. Jacques Piccard had begun working with the organization a couple of years earlier to make use of its expertise and resources, but now the navy bought the invention outright. Even though he no longer owned it, Piccard continued to work within the team of scientists on the *Trieste*, as it was now known, as they sought to reach their ultimate goal. The next couple of years brought repeated experiments at ever deeper levels as the vessel's upgraded cabin was tested to see if it could withstand the immense pressures involved. By January 1960, the team was ready.

The deepest known point in the world is in a gulf in the Pacific Ocean along the Mariana Trench called 'Challenger Deep'. On the morning of 23 January 1960, Jacques Piccard, accompanied by Donald Walsh, a US Navy Lieutenant, began the slow descent to this spot, seven miles below sea-level. It took several hours to complete the round trip to the bottom of the world and back again and, although, it was a success, it was not without incident. As the *Trieste* came to settle on the murky seabed, amazingly with some hitherto undiscovered deep-sea marine life coming into view at even these extreme depths, Piccard realised that the reinforced portholes were beginning to crack. Loss of the cabin's pressure or any entry of water at those depths would have resulted in instant death for the crew, so they very quickly began their ascent again. Fortunately, the windows held and Piccard literally lived to tell the tale in his book *Seven Miles Down*.

Although the journey to the bottom of the earth remained Jacques Piccard's ultimate achievement, he continued to carve out a distinguished career in submarine technology over the following decades. With his father he began developing a new type of vessel called a 'mesoscaphe', working to improve on its design and produce updated versions even after Auguste's death. Jacques envisaged that the submarine would eventually evolve into a mass underwater tourist vehicle but although thousands rode on a model in Lake Geneva during the Swiss National Exhibition in 1964, it remains a concept that is still to be fully exploited. Nevertheless, Piccard continued developing underwater inventions for the commercial industry over the following decades, as well as vessels for use in the scientific and research community.

While experiments continue and new designs are developed in these areas, few attempts have been made to re-examine the extreme depths that Piccard penetrated, much to his disappointment. 'We opened the door', he commented in later life. 'Now we must go and see what is behind the door.'

Neil Alden Armstrong *(1930–2012)*

After thousands of years of investigating the ends of the earth, perhaps the ultimate, and almost inevitable, exploratory feat would be to reach an object not even on it. Astronaut Neil Armstrong achieved that goal on 20 July

1969, the first man to set foot on the surface of the moon. A new chapter in the history of exploration had begun.

Mankind had been gazing at the moon in the night sky for millennia without seriously conceiving the prospect that it could ever be explored in person. Indeed, the human race had only just managed to reach both the top and the bottom of the earth in the immediate decades preceding Armstrong's historic flight, so it required a giant leap of faith even in the mid-twentieth century to believe that man would soon be standing on the moon.

Although the success of the Apollo 11 mission, which took Armstrong and his flight companions Edwin 'Buzz' Aldrin and Michael Collins to the moon, was the most obvious embodiment of man's aim to explore space, even this expedition was already benefiting from nearly a decade of manned space flights. If the lunar landing was the start of a new chapter in exploration's history, then those earlier missions constituted a significant prologue that made everything that followed, and will continue to follow for centuries to come, possible.

Not only was there an intense ideological rivalry between the United States and the Soviet Union throughout the 1950s and the 1960s, but there was also a space race. Both parties would soon have unmanned aircraft in orbit, but it was the Russians who wrote the most important opening paragraph in those early developments. For on 12 April 1961 they successfully sent cosmonaut Yuri Alexeyevich Gagarin into outer space, the first man to leave the immediate gravitational boundaries of the earth. They had beaten the Americans to a similar goal more than a hundred miles above the world's surface. Although it had taken the sixteenth century surface explorers years to circle the globe, within two hours Gagarin's *Vostok I* had 'circumnavigated' the entire earth in a single orbit and landed safely again in Russia.

With this psychological and physical boundary smashed, the concept of space exploration now gained full momentum. A new frontier was open to explorers and the first and most obvious target destination had to be the moon. Russia and America would continue to compete for this prize during the 1960s but, unfortunately, it was not one Gagarin himself was personally able to chase. Although he would have loved to complete this unprecedented 'double', the cosmonaut was killed in a mysterious air crash on 27 March 1968.

In the event, the American team won this time anyway. Yet, although it only took a few moments for Neil Armstrong to descend from his *Eagle* lunar module onto the surface of the moon with the now immortal words, 'That's one small step for man, one giant leap for mankind', it was years of personal preparation in the making.

Like many of the early space explorers, Armstrong had begun his career as an aviation pilot. After obtaining his flying licence at just sixteen years old, he went on to receive a scholarship from the navy. From 1949 to 1952 he was in the navy's service as an aviator, including a period spent flying nearly eighty sorties during the Korean War. On one occasion he was actually shot down, but survived to be rescued shortly afterwards. It would not be the only time Armstrong came close to death in his career in the skies.

By 1955, Armstrong had completed his Bachelor's degree in Aeronautical Engineering at Purdue University, which he would later supplement with a Masters from the University of Southern California, before continuing on his career path to space. He joined the National Advisory Committee for Aeronautics (NACA) in 1955, in its 'Lewis Flight Propulsion Laboratory'. This agency was a forerunner of the National Aeronautics and Space Administration (NASA) that later renamed Armstrong's department the 'Lewis Research Centre'. Armstrong eventually took a new posting with NASA'S 'High Speed Flight Station', where he augmented his already considerable flying experience piloting experimental aircraft. These included the X-15, which had a phenomenal top speed of 4,000 miles per hour. Close runs with death were a frequent occurrence in this occupation too, but nevertheless Armstrong survived to take his next 'small step' towards the moon when he became a fully fledged astronaut in 1962.

The American at last gained his 'space legs' in March 1966 aboard NASA's Gemini 8 mission. Although the assignment was a success in that it achieved the first docking between two orbiting vessels in space, it still had to be brought home early following complications. Yet again, however, Armstrong survived unscathed. During the 1960s he served in backup teams for a number of other US space operations before finally being told that he would lead the ultimate mission all astronauts sought.

There would still be one more scare before Armstrong

took his chance to depart for the moon, however. In May 1968, he had a near-fatal crash while undertaking practice exercises with a Lunar Landing Research Vehicle, but again he escaped.

After so many near misses, then, it was probably somewhat of a surprise that the Apollo 11 assignment successfully achieved its ground-breaking goal with no apparent threats on Armstrong's life. Launching on 16 July 1969, there was one slightly tense moment, however, as the *Eagle* lunar module came into land on the moon four days later. The team's landing site in the Sea of Tranquility turned out to be unexpectedly rocky, so Armstrong was forced to take manual control of the vessel and find a safe place to bring her down on the moon's surface. 'Houston', Armstrong reported, to confirm he had touched down safely, 'The *Eagle* has landed.'

Like so many exploratory feats over the previous centuries that were undertaken principally to satisfy national pride, the Apollo 11 team also found plenty of scientific justification for their expedition once they had landed. Over the next day, the crew dutifully collected samples and unpacked the research apparatus they had transported with them, before finally boarding again and safely heading for home.

The whole team were celebrated for their immense achievement on returning, but it was Armstrong above all, as the first man to step onto the lunar surface, who caught the public's imagination. Awards and plaudits were showered on him by countries and organisations around the world, in a manner that many of his earthly exploratory predecessors could only have dreamed of. His major achievement accomplished, however, the American was content to largely slip away from the spotlight, leaving NASA altogether in 1971 for a career in academia and, later, business.

The exploration of space remains in its infancy. Unlike the exploration of the earth, it is a task that will almost certainly never be completed because the distances involved, even in our own solar system, are beyond comprehension. In reality there is no final frontier; there is always another just beyond. Yet to the earliest human explorers, simply covering the world's surface, let alone its greatest heights or depths, would have seemed an equally unthinkable goal. By journeying to the ends of the earth, one piece, one mountain, one continent at a time, though, curious and determined men and women over the course of centuries have unveiled the world.

So while there remain unknowns, and there are an infinite number of them in the greater universe, the human race will continue whittling away at them, one small goal after another, quite simply just because they are there. The chronicles of exploration show above all else that the spirit of discovery is as old and as human as our species itself.

Acknowledgements & Further Reading

PRINT

Ambrose, Stephen E., *Undaunted Courage: Meriwether Lewis, Thomas Jefferson, and the Opening of the American West* (Rebound by Sagebrush, 1999)

Fleming, Fergus, *Barrow's Boys* (Granta Books, 2001)

Fleming, Fergus, *Ninety Degrees North: The Quest for the North Pole* (Granta Books, 2002)

Foster, Cliff, *Discovering the Boston Explorers* (Fen Press, 2003)

Matthew, H. C. G. (Editor) & Harrison, Brian Howard (Editor), *Oxford Dictionary of National Biography* (Oxford University Press, 2004)

Misc. *Baedeker's Australia* (AA Publishing, 2001)

Misc., *Collins World Atlas* (HarperCollins Publishers Ltd, 2003)

Misc., *Encyclopaedia Britannica* (Encyclopaedia Britannica (UK) Ltd, 2002)

Misc., *The "Times" Atlas of the World* (Times Books, 2002)

Monsarrat, Nicholas, *The Master Mariner* (House of Strauss, 2000)

Nuttall, Mark (Editor), *Encyclopedia of the Arctic* (Fitzroy Dearborn, 2004)

Prescott, Jerome, *100 Explorers Who Shaped World History* (Blue Wood Books, 1996)

Redmond, Sean, *The Journal of African Travel-Writing* (Number 3, September 1997, pp. 87-91).

Sattin, Anthony, *The Gates of Africa: Death, Discovery and the Search for Timbuktu* (Perennial, 2004)

Sobel, Dava, *Longitude* (Fourth Estate, 1998)

Welch, Galbraith, *The Unveiling of Timbuctoo: The Astounding Adventures of Caillie* (Carroll & Graf Publishers, 1991)

INTERNET

http://www.acs.ucalgary.ca
http://www.antarctica.ac.uk
http://www.bartleby.com
http://www.bbc.co.uk
http://christophercolumbus.org
http://www.cookpolar.org
http://www.nasa.gov
http://www.nationalgeographic.com
http://www.rgs.org
http://www.spri.cam.ac.uk
http://www.thebritishmuseum.ac.uk
http://www.un.org
http://www.wolfson.ox.ac.uk

Picture Credits